Some curious facts about how we make our living.

"Why didn't somebody tell us!"

by John L. Beckley

Illustrated by Jean Crane

Published by The Economics Press, Inc.
12 Daniel Road, Fairfield, N.J. 07006

All orders and inquiries should be addressed to The Economics Press, Inc.,
12 Daniel Road, Fairfield, N.J. 07006.

Copyright © 1982, The Economics Press, Inc., Fairfield, N.J. 07006.
Revised edition copyright © 1986, The Economics Press, Inc., Fairfield,
N.J. 07006.

ISBN 0-910187-00-2
Printed in the United States of America.

About The Author

As the Associated Press statistician, John Beckley created a daily business column called, "What the Figures Mean". Later he served as business editor of Newsweek Magazine, then started his own business, The Economics Press, developing and marketing training materials for industry.

One of Beckley's strengths, and perhaps weaknesses, as a writer is that he is totally unable to be wordy or long-winded. When the reader approaches a difficult subject he is gently picked up, carried directly through it with effortless logic, and deposited safely on the other side. By the time he realizes what has happened, Beckley is through—on to some other topic.

Fortunately, when it comes to economics, few people care to dawdle. Yet it's a complicated subject all of us should know a great deal more about. That's why this swift, one-way trip through economic history and our current economic problems will be a refreshing, welcome aid to many people.

Table Of Contents

Dear Peter:

Why would a man write a book about economic problems and address it to his grandson?

Perhaps because he knows, in the past at least, what a dull and tedious subject this has been. And I know I can't be dull and tedious with you. You won't listen if I am.

That sets me a high standard. Maybe if I can make a few facts about our economic life clear enough so that even a young fellow like you can easily understand them, a few other people may understand them better too.

Actually, there are few subjects the average person knows less about than economics. And few subjects about which people have picked up so much misinformation. Yet economics is vital to all of us. It's the study of how we make our living. We've been arguing about it ever since the dawn of history. How should we organize ourselves to work together? Who should get how much for doing what? Who should be the boss?

The economic system most of the free world operates under today is called private enterprise, free enterprise, or the profit system—three different names for the same thing. Some people don't like it. On the other hand, nobody anywhere has yet come up with a system that works anywhere near as well.

The thing people object to most is that profits are too big. Strangely enough, Peter, that is the very thing they know the least about. Not one person in a hundred has any idea how big profits really are, and how they compare with wages, salaries and other items. For years we've all heard a lot of talk that would lead us to think that profits MUST be BIG! But how big are they, really? Almost nobody knows!

If anyone doubts the truth of this statement, it is extremely easy to demonstrate. Just take the following four questions about profits and present them to anyone you would like to test. Insist that anyone who doesn't know the answers take a guess. The guesses they make will be extremely revealing.

Question No. 1: In the average company, which is bigger, employee compensation or profits? And how much bigger?

Answer No. 1: In the average company, employee

compensation is six times greater than profits. Six times as big.

Question No. 2: Out of every sales dollar a company takes in, how much goes into company profits?

Answer No. 2: A big supermarket, which doesn't need a lot of expensive machinery, usually makes a profit of less than one cent out of every dollar of sales. Less than 1¢ out of a $1.

A manufacturing company, which has a bigger investment in plant and equipment per dollar of sales, usually makes 4¢ to 6¢ profit on each dollar.

Question No. 3: How much of our National Income, what percent, is paid to employees?

Answer No. 3: Seventy-five percent of our National Income is paid out in compensation to employees. 75¢ out of every $1.

Question No. 4: How much of our National Income is paid out in dividends to stockholders?

Answer No. 4: Less than three cents out of every dollar of National Income is paid out in dividends to corporate stockholders. Actually, in the most recent year,

2.6¢ out of every $1.

I don't care what kind of people you present these questions to—students, professors, workers, teachers, even business executives—very few of them will have even one answer correct or close to correct. And in virtually every case, the errors will be on the side of grossly overestimating the size of business profits.

I'm sure there are many people who will read this to whom these figures will be absolutely unbelievable. I suggest they go to the library, get out the Statistical Abstract of the United States, and see for themselves.

How is it that so many of us grow up knowing so little about the fundamentals of the economic system by which we live? How can we be so uniformly sure that profits are so much bigger than they really are?

There are two reasons. One is that our educational system has been hard pressed to find adequate materials on this subject. It leaves us uninformed, unprepared to think rationally and to use good judgment in the area of economics. The other reason is propaganda. There are thousands and thousands of people, including influential writers, commentators, and professors, who are convinced that profits MUST be too big. They're so sure of it, in fact, that they have never stopped to investigate objectively. They just keep on talking. The rest of us can't help but listen now and then.

I hope, Peter, that your generation learns to think more clearly about economic problems than mine. Because what they think and believe, correct or incorrect, is going to shape the future of this country. Unless you make the right decisions, some of the wonderful values this country has developed and enjoyed may go down the drain. What are the right decisions? Lots of people have a lot of different opinions about that. I hope you'll take a good look at what lies down the road in all directions before you decide which way to go.

Meanwhile, take heart! I don't think you'll have the least bit of trouble understanding what I am talking about. Whether it makes sense or not you can judge for yourself.

What It's All About

ECONOMICS IS A study of how we make a living—how we satisfy our needs and wants.

The way we do it has been changing dramatically in the last 200 years. By comparison, in the 2000 years preceding that, it had changed hardly at all.

At the time of the Roman Empire, the only two industries of any importance were agriculture and war. That's what most of the people were engaged in. Most of mankind was having a difficult enough time getting enough to eat without worrying about anything else. A few individual journeymen made household wares, weapons, and tools but, compared with today, manufacturing didn't amount to a hill of beans. As a result, there weren't enough products to support much in the way of trade.

Land was the most important asset and the people who controlled the land usually controlled the government. They were the bosses and pretty much decided who got how much for doing what. There wasn't much the average person could do about it. He had to have land in order to raise food, and he had to have some protection against roving bands of marauders. The big landowner, who usually owned a big castle and had his own band of knights, gave him some protection in return for working the land.

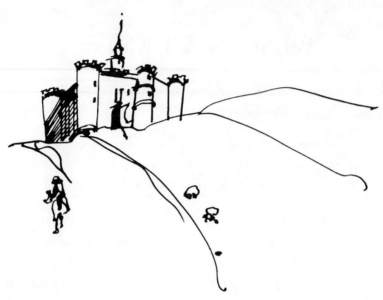

How much did the big landowner pay the serf or farmer? Usually as little as he had to. Just enough to keep him alive and working—unless by chance there was a shortage of labor. Sometimes, after a plague had wiped out a lot of the working people, the average peasant could make a little better deal for himself.

Where did the big landowners come from? How did they get to be landowners? Usually they got their land from the last warrior who conquered that section of the country. He became king, and his best friends, relatives, and associates became big landholders. And that's the way it went until somebody else conquered the territory. Whoever became king divided it up the way he felt like. People didn't argue with kings in those days unless they were very powerful nobles in their own right.

That's the way it went back then. The big land-owners had it made. They didn't have to work . . . neither did their families. Other people worked the land for them and got a small share in return. The peasants often objected that they were getting far too little but they weren't powerful enough to do anything about it. Votes didn't count in those days, just the force of arms. And kings and nobles were much more prepared to fight, and experienced at fighting, than ordinary people. The average person didn't even have any armor.

That's the way things were back in the Middle Ages. Things didn't change much from century to century because there was nothing to make them change. For more than a thousand years after the end of the Roman Empire the human race marked time. Production methods improved little, if at all. Everyone stayed just about as hungry and miserable as they had always been.

Then finally, and gradually, came the enlightenment. Men like Copernicus, Galileo, and Newton challenged the old theories of how the universe operated. Men started to navigate farther in ships . . . to the Far East . . . to America. Trade began to increase between various parts of the world. Manufacture was still primitive . . . entirely by hand and usually in household shops. But at least people were at last exchanging goods with one another . . . each country trading the things it was best at making for other goods somebody else could grow or make better than they.

Ultimately, over the centuries, the idea that kings should be the boss of everything began to weaken. One of the first challenges to the divine right of kings to rule as they pleased was the British House of Lords. At first this was still strictly for the most powerful landowners. Gradually, however, more and more of them were admitted. Eventually, a House of Commons also came into being to provide representation for people of lesser means.

The whole philosophy of government began to change, especially in England. For the first time the average man was considered to have some rights. Why? Simply because he was a human being. Furthermore, these rights were not to be arbitrarily interfered with. Any laws people were expected to obey should be clearly stated and approved in advance, and should apply equally to everyone. The government, furthermore, should avoid interfering with individuals as much as possible.

These developments, watched with great interest from across the Atlantic, led directly to the American Constitution and a new form of government for the United States. It was dedicated to protecting the rights of all citizens.

The Development of
Private Enterprise

As long as the conditions of life in Europe were dangerous, people preferred to live near a castle where they could flee in case of attack. As a result, the economy tended to be pretty simple. The castle owner usually owned the surrounding land as well, and he called the tune. You might get a bare living, or a little more—nobody except a very select few earned much in those days. But if you didn't like it, that was just too bad. There wasn't much you could do about it.

As conditions became safer, however, some of the people who had been fortunate enough, or thrifty enough, to buy or rent a piece of land began to sell their meat, grain, chicken, and vegetables in a nearby town. Craftsmen who made pots, pans, tools, and housewares gradually did the same.

That was the start of private enterprise. Nobody planned it; it just happened. People began to make or grow whatever they thought they could sell or trade, then buy other things somebody else could make better or cheaper than they did. The government had nothing to do with it. Individuals made what they felt like, bought what they felt like, and financed their own efforts. The only people annoyed by it were a few nobles who thought some of the common people were getting much too independent. The general attitude, however, was "laissez-faire" a French expression meaning "let it happen".

Private enterprise didn't happen only here or there. It was a natural, logical development of relations between men that happened all over Europe. Most trade was local, but gradually, as navigators found their way to other parts of the world, merchant vessels followed.

The amount of trade was limited, of course, by the fact that, in those days, we couldn't produce very much. Except for a few tools, and some very simple machines operated by manpower or horsepower, all the work of making things was done by hand.

Then, suddenly, came the dawn of a new age—the Industrial Revolution. It started in England just about the time we were fighting the American Revolution in this country. The British had already started building textile mills next to rivers in order to use waterpower.

Then a fellow named James Watt perfected an industrial steam engine which could be used to power industrial machinery anywhere. It made possible a tremendous increase in the output per worker.

Previously, because of the limited amount of crops and manufactured goods men could produce by hand, the average standard of living had edged up very slowly. Now, within the space of the next 200 years, the average American worker would be enjoying luxuries even a king would never have dreamed of.

Immediately people who saw the possibilities of new, steam-powered equipment began to get together to invest in new factories. The fabrics produced by the first factories were so much cheaper, the English realized they had discovered a bonanza. Almost immediately, they tried to keep it to themselves. In 1795 they passed laws to keep new machines, designs, or workmen who knew how to make them, from leaving the country.

Like most monopolies, however, it was an open invitation to others that here was a good thing. Before long the French, Germans, and other European nations had bought up enough British experts to have all the information they needed to compete. England was out in front in the race, however, and would lead it for more than 100 years, spreading its textiles, iron and steel, and machinery around the world.

All was not tranquil in England, however, especially with landed gentry, those people of inherited wealth who owned most of the countryside. By the early eighteen hundreds an entirely new group of wealthy people had appeared. They had made their money from new, fast-growing manufacturing businesses. What right did these people have to be making so much money, asked the estate owners. They were probably doing it by exploiting the poor or by dishonest methods of one kind or another!

The thing that really inflamed the landowners was the fact the manufacturers were urging that the Corn Laws be repealed or amended in order to provide cheaper food for their workers. The Corn Laws were a tariff on imported grain. Indirectly, they enabled English landowners to charge more for their grain too. Besides that, the growing demand for labor was forcing the big estates to pay more to keep workers on their farms.

Resentment of the new factories burst into flame in the 1820's and 1830's. London newspapers, controlled by the landowning families, began a vicious attack on the terrible working conditions and abuse of child labor in the new manufacturing enterprises. Eventually a Parliamentary committee was appointed to investigate the subject. All it did, however, was to hear testimony about the worst alleged abuses which had been reported or rumored over a considerable period of time. Then it closed the hearings and filed its report without giving the manufacturers a chance to answer.

It was a master propaganda stroke, one from which British manufacturers, and to some extent all manufacturers, have never fully recovered. Novelists, labor historians, and sociologists still use material from these hearings. Yet when the manufacturers finally managed to get them reopened two years later, and the original witnesses were recalled, they either recanted, or refused to swear under oath, to the truth of the testimony they had given.

The incident was typical, Peter, of many differences of opinion about economics. People on both sides get so worked up about their own point of view that they are apt to believe and promote any kind of smear which is good for their side, bad for the other. Each of us is influenced—sometimes prejudiced—by his own experience, sources of information, and his own emotional bent. That's why, before reaching any conclusions, it's wise to listen to all sides.

So what can we say, for sure, about working conditions in the early English factories? They certainly weren't the least bit like paradise. On the other hand, we suspect that every child who worked in one wasn't permanently stunted or deformed as a result. Some factory owners took excellent care of their workers, as good as was possible under the economic realities of that era. Other owners were as greedy and uncaring as they could get away with.

Some writers convey the impression that the men, women, and children who worked in the factories had previously been living an ideal existence in the beautiful English countryside. Then they were herded into factories by greedy manufacturers, shut off from the sunlight, and some of them chained to the machines.

That wasn't exactly the way it happened. The fact was that a good many of these men, women, and children had actually been starving in the countryside. England had become badly overpopulated. There were no more farm jobs available and hundreds of thousands of people had no way to make a living. Without the increase in factory jobs there would have been even wider hardship.

People went to work in factories because they welcomed any chance to work and to eat. And the pay was better than working on a farm or an estate. Those are pretty much the same reasons many people go to work in factories today. Factories are now, of course, much cleaner, safer, and more hygienic. Without them a vast part of our population too would have no way to make a living.

In England, the wave of resentment caused by the original Parliamentary hearings resulted in passage of The Factory Acts. These prohibited child labor in factories (but not on farms) and the new manufacturing movement faced a crisis. New, cheap labor was rushed over from Ireland, however, and the Industrial Revolution picked up speed again.

Ironically, the immediate casualties of the new law were the very children it was trying to help. They and their families now had less money to live on. That was more of a burden then than we can possibly appreciate today. Parental incomes, without the added income from working children, were often too small to keep families adequately clothed, housed, and fed.

Living conditions in the new factory areas were generally very poor. Many shacks had been put up in a hurry by workers themselves. Much of the rental housing had been built in haste in a period when England was still suffering from shortages of materials and labor caused by the Napoleonic Wars. Sanitary facilities and sewers were totally inadequate.

Bad housing, however, cannot be charged solely to the Industrial Revolution. Much of it was typical of the era. Conditions in the new tenements, much as the newspapers derided them, were no worse than those which had existed for hundreds of years, and still existed, in the London slums. Bad housing was nothing new; it wasn't invented by the Industrial Revolution. Furthermore, over a period of time, it was obvious that the increased productivity made possible by that revolution was the key factor in improving, not only housing, but all other living conditions of the average family.

Despite these problems, industrial production continued to spurt, not only in Great Britain, but in Western Europe, the United States and wherever civilization was exposed to western ideas. The standard of living of the average person, in all these areas, started upward and has continued upward almost uninterruptedly ever since.

A startling thing about it, Peter, yet something which is so obvious many people seem to forget it, is that the development of our industrial civilization, worldwide, was masterminded entirely by individuals. It was strictly and totally a product of *private enterprise.* No government planned it; no government was responsible for its success. Occasionally, a government would contribute a piece of land for a railroad or an incentive payment of some kind. In the total picture, however, these items have been so small as to be utterly negligible.

Except for Russia, parts of China and lesser communist countries, the worldwide industrial network which serves our needs has been built by individuals. They have risked their own money, time, and effort.

How did they manage to coordinate their efforts so well without some sort of overall plan? By the most practical method in the world—trial and error.

Under private enterprise each entrepreneur decides what products or services he thinks he can supply at a price that will interest customers. He invests in whatever plant and machinery he needs, hires workers, and starts to market the product. If it can be sold for more than it costs to make, hurrah! He's a success! He reinvests the profits, perhaps also borrowing more money, to build the business and profits as big as he can.

On the other hand, what if his guess proves wrong, and people don't want the new product? Or he can't sell it for enough to pay what it costs to make? He has to stop the business, pull the plug, and a wad of his capital goes down the drain.

That's how our national and international economies have developed in the past. Not by national planning and a decree: this is how we'll do it. Instead, we've done it by trial and error—success and failure of thousands of individual efforts. If something works, people do more of it. If it doesn't work, we stop. The consumers have been the ultimate bosses of everything. Whatever they want—if they're willing to pay what it costs, plus enough profit to interest some entrepreneur in risking his money to make it—that's what they'll get.

Entrepreneurs take thousands of risks every year in new businesses and old ones. Most new businesses fail in their first few years. But a few succeed, and some of them eventually grow into big businesses. That's what gives direction to the development of our economy.

That's one of the things that's wrong today, some critics say. Life, industry, and the world have gotten so complicated these days, they maintain, that we need national planning and national direction. Maybe so, maybe not, Peter. It may be, now that the world is bigger and more complicated, that we need individual management of our economic life more than ever. If we run our affairs by thousands of individual decisions, we can, over a period of time, eliminate the bad ones. Under national planning, one big, bad decision might eliminate us.

Trouble In Paradise

THROUGHOUT THE rest of the eighteen hundreds Great Britain rode a rising wave of prosperity. More and more factories were built. There were more jobs, more production, and British products were shipped around the world. British businessmen seemed to be making more money, year by year. The British workers were earning more and more too—their standard of living doubled in the first half of the century, then doubled again in the last fifty years. In the space of a hundred years, the average British worker was four times as well off as he had been. It was the great, prosperous Victorian era of British history.

Despite the general euphoria, however, serious criticism of private enterprise—otherwise known as the profit system—was beginning to build up in the background. The grumbling came, not from the workers as much as from the aristocracy and the intellectuals. The intellectuals were people who, generally speaking, were better educated and more sophisticated in things of the mind—ideas, theories, history, and philosophy. By occupation they included writers, artists, professors, clergymen, lawyers, and government employees.

A lot of these people felt that working to make profits was too selfish, too simple, and too grubby. There was nothing elevating or inspiring about it. Man didn't have to purify or control himself under this system. All he had to do was something that came naturally—be greedy.

The criticism was understandable. The profit system *was* absurdly simple—not the kind of thing that was apt to appeal to people who like complicated philosophies. And the main drive *was* selfishness or self-interest.

The criticism did, however, overlook or twist a few fundamentals. In order to make a profit, a person had to please, not himself, but a customer. The entrepreneur who pleased only himself would quickly go broke. In other words, the successful private enterpriser clearly had to be of service to others. Trying to make a profit was, in itself, no more greedy than working to get food, clothing, or shelter.

Simple, obvious systems may not be as challenging as those which are intricate and involved, but they usually tend to work better. The profit system was simplicity itself—direct, straightforward, and based on human nature as it actually was, not on human nature as someone dreamed it ought to be. The system was not designed. It *evolved* out of the actual experiences of people working and trading together.

Nevertheless, claimed the critics, it was obvious that business profits were *too big*. Too many people were getting rich at the expense of the workers and the public.

That, of course, was a matter of opinion. Nobody, in those days, knew how big profits actually were. Neither did they know how big profits *ought* to be in order to make the system work, in order to encourage a growing investment in tools, equipment, and factories.

Most people did not realize then—and many still do not recognize today—that every advance in our standard of living requires an additional investment in productive equipment. We constantly need more and better tools and equipment in order to produce more goods. Otherwise we start to slide backward. Our investment per worker has increased, sometimes faster, sometimes slower, ever since the start of the Industrial Revolution. That's the essential reason why each generation has been better off than the one preceding it. At least part of the seed money comes from profits. It is reinvested in industry because of the prospects and hope of more profits in the future.

Nevertheless, the charge that profits are "too big" remains, even today, a serious challenge to private enterprise. It's not a factual argument. Nobody presents statistics showing exactly how big profits *ought* to be and why. It tends to be a prima facie case. The rich are too rich, the poor are too poor, and, therefore, profits are too big. Whether there is any logic to it or not doesn't seem to matter. It is the most powerful argument against private enterprise today. If it succeeds—for the wrong reasons—we may all pay a severe penalty.

One of the intellectuals who thought capitalism was not merely unfair but positively evil was Karl Marx. Capitalism, of course, is another name for the system we've been talking about. Call it private enterprise, free enterprise, the profit system, or capitalism, they all refer to the same thing. Capitalism has become the nastiest word, however, implying an emphasis on money and greed.

Marx was a German sociologist and philosopher whose ideas got him into trouble with the German government. So he emigrated to England where he continued his work, staying in touch with revolutionary and "advanced" thinkers on the continent.

Marx was a strange contrast. His vision of correcting man's defects and achieving a perfect society on earth stimulated intellectuals tremendously. Yet when his followers tried to apply those ideas to human beings, he was indirectly responsible for the torture and death of millions of people. Marxist thinking is at the core of virtually every revolutionary movement in the world today.

Marx was an idealist and an extremist. He was convinced that most of our troubles in this world are caused by the fact that man is an intensely selfish, self-centered animal. We are so interested in owning things that our economy and our government have been developed primarily to protect private property. That, said Marx, was the source of our troubles.

Private enterprise, he declared, exploited the average man, the "proletariat", for the benefit of the rich. The owners of businesses, by insisting on a profit, were taking away gains that rightfully belonged to the workers. Capitalism, he said, had no interest in the worker other than milking him for every last bit of energy and labor. The capitalists, he declared, would *never* pay workers more than barely enough to keep them alive and reproduce themselves to provide workers for the future.

What was needed, said Marx, was a worldwide revolution of the workers. To achieve results, it would have to be ruthless and bloody. Then a dictatorship of the proletariat which would eliminate private property and remake men into selfless, social animals. Eventually, as man became less selfish, the need for government would completely disappear. Men would be at peace with each other; there would be paradise on earth.

A beautiful picture, a glorious prospect. Unfortunately, the experiments with Marxism haven't worked out that way. Not yet, anyhow. Perhaps with a few more centuries, or thousands of years, of pain and suffering, they will. For that, however, we'll have to wait and see, and I don't expect either of us to be around that long.

I have been trying to think, Peter, as I sit here at the typewriter, if there is any area of the world today which is happier or better off because of Marxism. Marxism, incidentally, is the political philosophy of Communism.

If there is, I cannot think of it. Some Communist countries have special tours which show off a few of their accomplishments to visitors. In none of them, however, can you walk in, look over the country at leisure, then make up your mind the way you can in the United States. They all have hidden or forbidden areas into which visitors cannot go. The things we see are special exhibits. I'm afraid the grim truths lie hidden elsewhere. Perhaps, in time, this will not be the case. But let's wait for more evidence before we think of buying the idea.

Marx, of course, was wrong about a number of things; most theoreticians are. One of the most obvious was his belief that capitalists would *never* pay workers more than just enough to live on. Yet, as we've seen, the standard of living of British workers doubled in the first half of the 19th century. Then it doubled again in the second half.

What happened? The capitalists didn't suddenly become more generous. Competition *forced* them to give workers a larger share. Competition for labor to man new factories forced wages upward. At the same time, greater productive efficiency was forcing costs and prices down. Competition in the market meant cheaper goods for the British worker. Labor not only had more to spend—it was getting more for its money.

Defects in Marx's thinking, however, didn't affect the popularity of his ideas in the least. He had created an appealing ideological basis for dissatisfaction and revolution wherever men owned private property, wherever the means of production were in private hands. Hate the boss! Hate the rich owners! They're cheating you!

To anyone who doesn't own much property—and that includes most of the people in this world—that's a very tempting idea. That's why the rich have so much and we have so little—they've been cheating us! And how can anyone prove otherwise? The average man doesn't understand enough about economics to even follow the argument. Besides, he'd much rather believe he's been treated unfairly.

It takes emotion, not reason, to build a strong popular movement—something to hate and something to love. Marx taught his followers to hate property and profits. But he also gave them something to love: that beautiful society of the future where all men would share equally in everything, where laws and government would be totally unnecessary.

How this paradise would be achieved, Marx never explained. Somehow, the dictatorship of the proletariat would take care of that. All that was necessary was for human beings and human nature to be redesigned and remade. Then everything would be wonderful.

The movement developed some appealing slogans. Like "production for use instead of for profit" or "from each according to his abilities, to each according to his needs". These, if you don't think about them too critically, sound rather impressive. But production for profit is, obviously, production of the things people want most. That's why it's profitable. What, then, is production for use? Is it production of something people may not want, but we think they better have it anyway?

And if you give a man the same reward for his best efforts as for an average effort, the whole history of mankind shouts that he is not going to keep giving you top performance—not for long anyway. Most human beings respond to incentives and disincentives, encouragement and discouragement. And they always will, even if and when communists control the whole world.

The Socialists

THE MARXISTS, of course, weren't the only ones who objected to the way the world was developing. A lot of intellectuals had begun toying with the idea of socialism—have the government own the means of production and run the economy. Philosophers wrote books about it, some suggesting that all income be divided equally among everyone. Other would-be socialists were more reserved. They thought incomes should be *more* equal but not necessarily *exactly* the same for everyone. But who should decide who should get how much for doing what? Aside from those who believed all incomes should be equal, they never got around to deciding that question. That, for the time being, would be left to the future.

The kind of economy the socialists wanted was no different from that of the Marxists. But they didn't want a bloody revolution and a dictatorship of the proletariat in order to get it. They preferred to proceed peacefully, constantly educating people to the idea, until they had a majority which could take over the government.

Socialist parties promoting this viewpoint began springing up in various countries. One of the most famous in the later nineteenth century and continuing on into the twentieth were the Fabians in England. A group of intellectuals, writers, and aristocrats, they created a steady series of papers purporting to show how socialism could be applied to this industry or that, eliminating profits and taking control into the hands of the government.

The famous dramatist, George Bernard Shaw, was a Fabian and wrote a special book about socialism for women. He was so sure of his views, and so convincing a writer, that it virtually sweeps one off his feet. Yet frankly, Peter, the idea of George Bernard Shaw proposing absolutely equal incomes for everyone, which he did, tickles my funny bone. He was such an elegant, conceited person that I just cannot visualize him being content to be average in any possible way. He did weaken to the extent of allowing that it might not hurt to have a few larger incomes for special performers like singers and writers. In his case, his plays are so wonderful, I certainly wouldn't object, would you?

Russian Communism

THE WORLD WAS moving on into the twentieth century. Production and industry continued to grow everywhere under the impetus of private enterprise. Wages continued to buy more and more of the necessities and luxuries of life.

In Europe, however, change was in the wind. The Marxists were indoctrinating, planning, and plotting, especially in Russia. Socialist parties had appeared in most of the parliaments of Europe and were gradually increasing in influence. Suddenly, all was upset by World War I which swept Europe from 1914 through 1918.

In Russia, in 1918, as the Czar's war effort collapsed, his government collapsed around him. The Czar resigned, leaving a power vacuum waiting to be filled. Into this opening stepped a brilliant intellectual and ruthless man of action, Nicholai Lenin.

Lenin had been planning for and dreaming of this kind of opportunity for more than 20 years. He was a devout Marxist, had been since his teens, and recognized it as the perfect philosophy for promoting and continuing revolution. Even though Lenin and his Bolsheviks were a minority party, they moved into the breech ruthlessly, seizing power without hesitation and without waiting for the approval of anyone. Within three years they had the country totally under their control, ready for remaking in the Marxist pattern.

Marx created the economic philosophy of the Communist State. Lenin designed and developed a power structure to control that state. The monster he created, which has never been challenged, is still in absolute, unquestioned power. It frightens me, Peter, more than anything Marx ever said or wrote. Even if they dropped the Marxist philosophy entirely, that power structure would still be a dangerous threat to every man who believes in personal liberty. The fact that it is a power openly dedicated to world revolution makes it even more so.

The whole basis of government in the U.S.S.R. is

exactly the opposite of what it is in the United States. In the United States all power comes up from the people. If the American people don't like something the government does, they can eventually reverse it. In Russia, all power comes down from the top. The government doesn't need or ask anyone's approval to do anything. There are no safeguards to interfere with the government officials doing what they please with anybody. The individual has no rights; if he doesn't do whatever the government wants him to, he's interfering with the revolution.

A vital instrument in government power is the Communist Party. It consists of only a few million members, all thoroughly indoctrinated in Marxism and the Communist philosophy. There are no half-way, or doubtful members, or independent thinkers. If they don't believe according to the book, and follow instructions to the letter, they are *out*. The party is not an instrument for shaping the ideas of the government. It is an instrument for shaping and spying on the ideas of the people.

People don't dare associate freely with one another in the Soviet Union. The only groups who meet together are officially authorized, and supervised by party members, usually for the purpose of government supervision and propaganda. People are kept separated from one another so that organized revolt or resistance is simply out of the question. Even normal, friendly human relations can be very difficult.

Lurking behind the scenes at all times is the secret police. They are the government's special instrument for intimidating anybody. They don't have to worry about Congressional opinion or the rights of citizens, like the FBI does in the United States. They can arrest, grill, torture, and kill or exile anyone except, perhaps, the overall dictator of the moment.

I wish I were exaggerating, Peter, but I am afraid there is more than ample evidence to support everything I have said. For more than sixty years the Communist government has been trying to organize industry and agriculture on a state owned, state operated basis. It has tortured, starved, killed, and exiled millions of people in this effort. Yet so far it hasn't been able to produce a standard of living which even comes close to that of the more backward countries which practice private enterprise.

One thing, however, it has done. By devoting its most able people to armaments, and concentrating on that one goal, it has become the most heavily armed nation in the world. The Russian Government does not have to ask people to approve big arms budgets. The arms budget comes first; people have to make do with what's left.

The Growth Of
Socialist Thinking

THE SOCIALISTS, after World War I, were gaining ground throughout Europe. They have continued to do so right up to the present moment. They have, however, had a few new things to worry about that bothered some of their better thinkers.

Why was it, for example, that state ownership and operation of industry and agriculture were working so poorly in Russia? Russia had tremendous natural resources and a talented people. Could it be that socialism wasn't as productive as private enterprise? Or were the poor results of socialism in Russia caused by the effort to tie in a social revolution, and to change the very nature of man? Would socialism have worked better if the government had been more reasonable, less ruthless and dictatorial? If it hadn't tried to change so many things at once? No one could answer those questions conclusively either way.

Another thing which shook the confidence of socialist intellectuals—who tended to be kindly, generous people personally—was the cruelty and horror of the National Socialist movement in Germany. Did this mean that whenever a socialist government took over control of an economy there would be violence, dictatorship, and an end to the rights of the individual?

One of the people who feared this was Friedrich A. Hayek, a prominent Austrian economist who later won the Nobel Prize. Hayek had grown up on the continent, but when Hitler came to power, he was living in England teaching at the University of London. Hayek was appalled by what was happening in Germany. He was equally shocked, however, by the attitudes of his intellectual friends in England. They were the identical attitudes which had preceded collectivism and National Socialism in Germany.

In 1944 Hayek expressed his fears in a book called, "The Road to Serfdom". It angered many socialists and disturbed others. Dedicating his book to socialists of all parties, Hayek pointed out how socialism might lead to tyranny and the death of individual freedom.

Under private enterprise the production of goods is planned by thousands of entrepreneurs operating independently. They are each guided by prices and profits. Each is trying to create and produce goods the consumer wants badly enough to pay a fair price for. What's a fair price? From the entrepreneur's point of view, it's enough so he can cover his costs and make a profit. If he doesn't think he can make a profit, he doesn't produce anything.

But prices and profits depend on a market system, a free exchange of goods and services. Without such a system, the government has to run the show. It has to plan what will be produced and how it will be divided up. And that's no small job. It's such a colossal, impossible job, in fact, that even after 60 years of socialism, Russia's economy is still a mess—bumbling, inefficient, and totally snarled in red tape.

Without a profit system, how do you know what to produce? In order for any plan to work, Hayek pointed out, the planners must have the power to carry it out. People must act the way it has been planned for them to act. When a plan doesn't work, the most likely excuse is that it hasn't been enforced strongly enough. What's needed is more power, more affirmative action. Soon individual rights don't matter at all. All that matters is the welfare of society as a whole.

People who seize power at times like these, Hayek feared, will not be gentlemanly, friendly, intellectuals. They will be demagogues and revolutionists like Hitler and Lenin who know how to mobilize people through hate and terror. "Hate profits" "Hate the kulaks" "Hate the Jews". These are the kind of slogans which have been used to muster support for successful socialist movements in the twentieth century. Hayek is fearful that such appeals may be essential to a broadly supported socialist movement. Socialism masquerades under the name of brotherhood, but rallies support through hate, greed, and nationalism. Hayek claims it automatically brings the worst to the top.

Was Hayek right? Nobody really knows for sure, Peter. The jury is still out. His book definitely made a lot of socialists stop to think things over. The socialist trend has continued and socialist majorities now control most of the countries of free Europe. But, despite their avowed belief in socialist principles, not one of them has yet thrown private enterprise totally out of the window.

Instead, a new trend has appeared, the welfare state. It's a new approach to the same goal—sharing the wealth. The thinking behind it is something like this: if the market economy is so efficient, why not leave it alone? Let it continue to operate. But tax away most of the profits and big incomes and use them for public purposes. Leave the productive system alone, but share the wealth it produces. Spread the goodies around through all sorts of government benefit programs.

This is the path we've been following in the United States. Ever since the New Deal of the thirties we've been creating more and more giveaways at government expense to take care of more and more human needs.

What's wrong with that? Maybe nothing; maybe a great deal. Can we afford all of these programs, and more to come, without a runaway inflation? Are they administered in a way that builds character or destroys it? How much do we pay for them in hidden taxes and inflation, and are they really worth it?

Because of higher taxes on medium and higher incomes, we're not building up business capital as rapidly as we used to. Money which was formerly saved and invested in new equipment and jobs is being taxed away and used for benefit programs. That isn't good, Peter, no matter how worthy the benefits may sound. It's something we can't get away with too long without paying the price.

We'll talk more about problems like these later. For the moment, let's just celebrate the fact that our discussion is finally up-to-date. We're at last talking about things that are happening here and now. Our quick trip through economic history—perhaps the fastest on record—was intended to give you a better background for understanding current problems.

First Let's Talk About Money

HOW DOES ONE discuss economic problems? Is there any such thing as a natural order? I'm afraid there isn't. So let's just go ahead, taking up one area after another where I know there has been considerable misunderstanding. After we consider the most obvious problems, we'll look around and see what's left.

One of the things you have to understand if you want to deal intelligently with economic problems is money. What it is and what it isn't.

Money is most commonly used in two ways. One is as a medium of exchange. The other is as a place to keep purchasing power until you want to use it.

Instead of trading one piece of merchandise for another, like alarm clocks for pork chops, or overcoats for radios, we exchange whatever we want to sell for money. Then we use that money, all or part of it, to buy whatever we want. Using money as a medium of exchange is a lot more convenient than bartering. Our civilization couldn't exist without it.

Also, if you've got some things you don't want right now—perhaps they might spoil or go out of style—you sell them for money. Then you keep the money until there's something you want to use it for. Money is a place to store wealth or value until you want to spend it.

At least money's *supposed* to be a good place to store value. And it is, unless the Government starts increasing the money supply. When the Government increases the money supply, prices go up and money isn't worth what it used to be. When prices are rising sharply, money is not a good place to store value at all.

Centuries ago, gold, silver, jewelry, and other precious metals were used as money. As a medium of exchange, sometimes these weren't too convenient. When you're trading with diamonds as money, for example, how do you make change?

As a store of value, however, these items were excellent. They were scarce and precious. And the supply couldn't be increased just by turning on a printing press.

Some of the precious metals were turned into coins. The difficulty was that whenever an emperor or king was running out of money he would *debase the coinage.* He would make coins out of less pure alloys, or cheaper metal, and declare they had the same value as the old.

The Roman Empire, for example, had a copper coin called the *As.* Heavily in debt because of the war with Carthage, the Romans reduced the copper content of the *As* from twelve ounces to a half an ounce. Then they used the new coins to pay off their old debts. This wiped out the savings of most Roman citizens.

This happened so often in the Roman Empire—the cheating of citizens by their own government—that some historians believe it was a major factor in the decline and fall of that empire. The people, defrauded again and again, eventually lost all faith in their government.

In the modern world we have gradually progressed from metals to paper. For a while there were a number of paper moneys partially backed by gold and silver— so-called gold and silver certificates.

That kind of money is virtually gone now. Nowadays money, except for small change, is almost always paper. It is printed exclusively by various governments which declare it to be legal tender. That means it has to be accepted in payment of debts.

In other words, if the ticket on the merchandise says $2.00, the merchant *has* to accept those two green pieces of paper you have in your hand that are marked as $1 bills. They are legal tender. But if he doesn't think the money is much good, if there is too much of it floating around, he doesn't have to keep his price at $2.00. Next year the same item may cost $4.00.

That's the principal trouble with paper money. Governments simply can't be trusted not to print more money if they need it to help pay their bills. That includes the good old U.S.A., a Government we like to think of as by the people, for the people, and of the people. Nowadays it also hoodwinks the people by increasing the money supply and constantly lessening the buying power of the dollar.

Next — Inflation

WHILE WE'RE TALKING about money, we might as well talk about inflation. Inflation is a decline in the purchasing power of money. The prices of everything go up. The same item that used to cost you $1.00 now costs $2.00. It's an old, old story—as old as money itself.

Whenever you have a serious inflation, you can be sure one of two things happened, perhaps both of them:

1. A big expansion in DEMAND caused by an increase in the supply of money and credit.

2. A substantial increase in production COSTS.

Which of these is the most important? Almost invariably the increase in money and credit. *Every significant inflation in history has been preceded and accompanied by a big expansion in money and credit.* Invariably, what starts it is a government that wants to spend more money than it can collect—or has the courage to collect—in taxes. So they debase their metal currency to create more money. Either that or print more paper money and call it legal tender.

To understand how inflation happens, you have to know a few things about money and banking. Not a lot—just a little, and it's not that difficult.

A word of warning—when we talk about the money supply here, we don't mean just paper money. What we mean is money and credit—all the purchasing power people have readily available to use in the market to buy the things they need and want.

That includes cash, the deposits in your bank accounts, and the amount you can charge using credit cards. In this day and age, checks and credit cards are just as spendable as cash. All of these are purchasing power which can be reflected in the demand for products and services anytime people are in the mood.

The marvelous—and sometimes unfortunate—thing about banks is, that whenever a bank makes a loan, it increases the money supply. Even a plain ordinary personal loan to you or me.

Banks can expand the supply of money and credit so easily it seems like sleight of hand. To see precisely how it happens, let's slow it down a bit and take it step-by-step.

To begin with, Peter, let's suppose that you and I are running the banking system in a small country. One day some businessmen come in to one of our banks and want to borrow $1,000,000. In order to do it, we just turn on the accounting machine and credit $1,000,000 to their checking accounts. Now they can write checks to pay bills or come in and draw out cash for the payroll—they can use the $1,000,000 any way they want to.

But don't forget this: the minute we credited that $1,000,000 to their deposit accounts, the deposits in our bank (and the nation's money supply) increased by $1,000,000. And that $1,000,000 won't disappear just because they spend it. If they use it to pay off suppliers, the $1,000,000 will show up immediately in suppliers' bank accounts when they deposit the checks. If cash is taken out and used for payrolls, most of it will reappear in increased deposits by merchants where employees spent the money. Some of the cash may be added to the hoard under somebody's mattress.

But please remember this: the $1,000,000 of increased purchasing power we created by making that loan has not disappeared. It is still around somewhere, part of our money supply. *The added purchasing power will continue to exist until that loan (or some other $1,000,000 loan) is repaid.*

That's how bank loans—ordinary, everyday bank loans—inflate the money supply. The expansion of bank credit—which increases bank deposits and the money supply—is a tremendously important factor in inflation.

Fortunately, loans that help businesses expand their output are not as inflationary as some other loans. The increased purchasing power created by these loans is at least partially offset by growth in the supply of goods and services the loans make possible.

Consumer credit is a horse of a different color. Consumer credit enables people to spend more money than they would otherwise, clearly increasing the *demand* for goods rather than the supply. As far as any one individual is concerned, this effect is temporary. Loans and credit cards may help him buy more for a while, but sooner or later he has to cut back and live within his income.

What prevents banks from increasing their loans and deposits indefinitely? The reserve balance requirements of the Federal Reserve. Every bank has to keep a certain percentage of its deposits with the

Fed—usually somewhere between 3% and 12%.

Once a bank's deposits have risen to the point where its reserve balances with the Fed are barely adequate, it can't make any more loans without breaking the law. More loans would increase its deposits and require it to keep larger reserves with the Fed. It doesn't have the money.

One way a bank can get around this is to borrow money from another bank or from the Federal Reserve itself. When the Fed is trying to prevent further inflation, however, such loans may be very expensive.

Fortunately, businesses and individuals can't keep on increasing their borrowing forever. Eventually their loans have to be repaid, or at least kept in a reasonable relationship to the borrower's means.

In this country there is only one organization which can keep on expanding the money supply by borrowing and borrowing, more and more, year after year. That organization is the Federal Government—and that's exactly what it has been doing for the last fifty years. During those same fifty years we've had the only sustained, uninterrupted inflation in the history of our country.

Why are government deficits so inflationary? Because government spending rarely increases the supply of goods people want to buy. All it does is increase the money supply.

The Federal Reserve Bank is the tool which the Federal Government uses to borrow more money every year to cover its deficits. When the Government wants to borrow, the Federal Reserve creates whatever additional money and credit is needed to handle the situation.

The Federal Government's credit is always good— the best. Why? Because anytime it wants to borrow, the Federal Reserve Bank will give it credit and print more paper money if necessary. And that paper money has to be accepted by everyone in the country. It's legal tender.

When the Federal Reserve Bank was created in 1913, one of its most important functions, supposedly, was to prevent financial panics and runs on banks. The idea was that anytime a bank was running out of cash it could pledge some of its assets with the Federal Reserve and get more. The Federal Reserve was given the right to extend credit and print new money to whatever extent was necessary to do the job.

The Fed has done exactly that—but not because it was needed to stop financial panics. Instead, ever since the New Deal of the 1930's, it has created the money and credit needed by a government and a Congress committed to increased spending and huge deficits year after year.

This constantly increasing supply of money and credit has created the excess DEMAND which keeps prices moving up.

Let's suppose, Peter, that your school cafeteria was unexpectedly closed one noontime. Nobody was prepared for it, but one boy happened to have a bag of ten candy bars in his locker. Now let's also suppose that every kid in school had a couple of dollars in change in his pocket. Some of them would be offering him more for a candy bar, wouldn't they, than they would if each of them only had a dime?

That's the way our economic system works. When the money supply goes up, but the supply of goods doesn't, prices go up too. Prices are like Ping-Pong balls floating in a tub of water. The water in the tub represents the nation's buying power. Every time you raise the water level (by pouring in more money and credit), the balls float higher in the tub. Borrowing to pay for federal deficits has been pouring water into this tub for the last 50 years, recently in larger and larger quantities. And prices, in the last decade, have been moving up faster than ever.

For our first 150 years, this country lived within its income. Except for rare emergencies, we balanced the budget, on the average, almost every year. It was a ritual we, the people, believed in. We didn't think it was right for our country—or anybody—to spend more money than they took in. As a result our country never had a serious inflation except in time of war.

The emergency spending deficits of the New Deal somehow changed all that. Those deficits didn't bankrupt the country. Or even seem to matter much. So why not loosen up the belt? Soon deficit spending was a habit. The result has been growing inflation, year after year.

The other thing which can cause serious inflation is a substantial increase in production costs. This is usually the result of big, persistent wage increases, wage increases which far exceed any increase in efficiency and productivity. Such wage increases *have* to be passed along to consumers in the form of higher prices. If business organizations had to absorb these wage increases, their profits would soon disappear and so would they. Nobody stays in business to make a loss. People go into business solely to make a profit. When that's impossible, they shut down.

Wages and employee benefits are a big factor in business costs. In the average firm they are more than six times as big as profits. So how could big, repeated wage increases possibly come *out* of profits? Obviously they can't. They have to be passed along in higher prices.

One of the most damaging misconceptions of the last 50 years is that people ought to have wage increases every year, and that these wage increases *can* be paid out of profits. We've witnessed a continuing thrust by labor and government supposedly to get workers a larger share of the profits of business enterprises.

In one respect at least, they have succeeded. There have been thousands of wage increases year after year. Wages today are several times as big as they used to be.

BUT THOSE WAGE INCREASES DIDN'T COME OUT OF PROFITS. THEY COULDN'T HAVE COME OUT OF PROFITS. Profits aren't big enough to provide such wage increases and never have been in the average corporation.

Wages and other employee compensation have always been at least 6 or 7 times as big as profits. And profits haven't disappeared. They are still taking approximately the same share of sales dollar as they used to.

Then where *did* the wage boosts come from?

They came from two places. Some of the wage increases were paid for by greater productivity; the rest were passed along to customers in the form of higher prices.

Greater productivity—whether it is achieved by working harder, smarter, or with better tools and equipment—is the source from which all material blessings flow. It cuts costs and we get more product for less money. That makes possible better wages, lower prices, or bigger profits. Any wage boosts which can't be paid for by greater efficiency have to be added to the price of the product.

If a new machine enables a worker to produce 1,000 bottles an hour instead of 500 (and the machine doesn't cost too much more than the old one), that's an increase in productivity. The company can afford to pay the worker higher wages, charge the customer lower prices, or make bigger profits—maybe a little bit of all three.

Everybody's in the same boat—labor and capital alike. In order to have more, we've got to produce more. There is no other way.

One of the major problems of our country today is that so many millions of people have been encouraged to expect more and more every year, often for doing less and less. The truth is that anyone who gets more without producing more is getting it at the expense of all the rest of us. The rising cost of his or her services is part of the inflation we're suffering from.

How Big Should Wages And Profits Be?

UNDER A free-enterprise system, neither wages nor profits need to be controlled. They should be as high or as low as free competition makes them. The market speaks for you, me, and everyone else.

One of the great advantages of the profit system is that it encourages production of those things people want most, and discourages production of those things we want least. If we want the benefits of a profit system, we have to leave profits and wages free to fluctuate whatever way the market dictates. The higher the level of profits and wages in any industry, the more it encourages new companies and new workers to enter it. When competition gets too tough, and profits and wages fall, people and companies start deserting the business to try something else.

When anyone attempts, arbitrarily, to decide what profits *ought* to be, he is interfering with the MARKET. *And there's no record that anyone, anywhere, who attempted to do this has ever achieved desirable results for any appreciable length of time.* The odds are overwhelmingly against it.

The MARKET isn't always right, but it's more apt to be right than any individual or any Government agency. And when it's wrong, competition corrects it very quickly. You may not like the price you have to pay for the things you need and want, but you can be sure there are good reasons for those prices—maybe a hundred reasons you're not aware of. When the Government tries to decide what prices, profits, or wages *ought* to be, we always get into trouble one way or another.

Why Price Controls Don't Work

IF WE WANT to stop inflation, why not try something obvious like price controls? Public opinion polls occasionally show that's what a majority of the people think we ought to try. So why don't we?

The best reason is that price and wage controls don't work. They simply aren't practical. Governments have been trying to control prices for more than four thousand years. Nobody has ever been successful at it except for very brief periods. Then, when the controls had to be abandoned, prices went right back to where they would have been anyway.

If you have a little time, and you'd like to verify this, pick up a copy of FORTY CENTURIES OF WAGE AND PRICE CONTROLS by Robert Schuettinger and Eamonn Butler. The stories they tell about futile efforts to control prices and wages all over the world are fascinating.

In ancient Egypt price and wage controls were so deeply resented that workers and landowners ran away from their farms. The Government had to take them over. Eventually the whole economy collapsed.

The Roman Empire made repeated attempts to control prices and wages. None were successful. One of the most interesting was the effort made by the Emperor Diocletian in the third century A.D.

Diocletian came to power after a prolonged period of inflation. So he established a brand new currency and put out an edict establishing fixed prices and wages for more than 1,000 different commodities and kinds of labor. There were widespread riots and thousands of people were killed in the effort to enforce these regulations.

Enforcing the regulations created so many problems that four years later Diocletian abdicated. In those four years the price of gold, in terms of Roman currency, had increased 250 percent. In spite of Diocletian's efforts, prices were still soaring.

Fifteen centuries later, after the French Revolution, the new French Government tried four different price control schemes in less than two years. None of them worked.

Why don't price and wage controls work?

There are two reasons. One is that they aggravate the very problem they are trying to correct. Rising prices are usually caused by shortages. There isn't as much of the commodity available as people would like to buy. So the price starts going up.

If you leave the price alone, the higher price may help increase the supply. On the other hand, if controls stop the price from going up, perhaps even force it down a bit, people lose interest in producing the item. The shortage gets worse. In price-controlled markets, the supply dwindles, perhaps even disappears. In illegal, black markets the price goes higher than ever.

The other reason price and wage controls don't work is human nature, and human nature today isn't much different than it was in ancient Rome. Almost everyone directly affected by price or wage controls—then or now—feels he is being cheated and treated unfairly.

How would you feel if you were forced to sell something you owned for less than you knew it was worth? Or if you were forced to work for less than you knew someone else would gladly pay you?

And how would you feel if you wanted to buy something very badly and you were perfectly willing to pay the price the seller asked for it, but the Government wouldn't let you pay that much?

These feelings reappear whenever and wherever price and wage controls are applied. And they are very powerful. They lead to resistance, violence, and black markets.

The two places where controls have come closest to working are Nazi Germany and Russia, both places where people's lives were, or are, tightly regimented. Neither was or is a free market.

Toward the end of World War II prices in Nazi Germany seemed under fairly good control. Most goods were strictly rationed, however, and the result was people had money they couldn't spend. There was also an active black market in many items despite Nazi controls.

In Russia, prices seem to be relatively stable—official prices that is. But if you want attention and prompt service, it takes extra payments to get it. There is also a parallel, or black market in many, many items in case you want more than you can get at the regular price with your ration tickets.

If we want to operate this country like a prison, we might have some luck with controls for a while. But it's just a question of time before it will be obvious that they don't work and ought to be junked.

Price controls distort the economy; they upset the price signals which normally guide men, materials, and money into making the things we want and need most. They also waste an enormous amount of manpower simply to administer them. Nevertheless they seem like such a direct, appealing solution to the problem of inflation that governments keep trying them again and again.

What It Takes To Stop Inflation

THE MOST effective way to stop inflation is to correct the things which are causing it. In our case, this means, primarily, two things: (1) stopping the Government deficits which expand the money supply, and (2) stopping wage increases which exceed the increase in productivity.

It's not only the most effective way, Peter—I'm afraid it's the only way. Anyone who thinks differently, be he President, politician, economist, or labor leader, is asking for trouble. All history and logic are against him. If we don't stop these two forces, inflation will keep right on inflating. Price increases, sometimes slower, sometimes faster, will be with us forever.

Unfortunately, government spending programs, once started, never seem to taper off or decline. The people always seem to want more. The groups who benefit, even though in the case of some programs they are a small minority, are strongly organized. If a Congressman votes against a program that benefits them, they'll propagandize against him and vote against him.

The great majority, who don't benefit from a specific program, are seldom that concerned. That's why it's so hard to make any real headway in cutting Federal spending.

All government programs have worthy objectives. That's why Congressmen keep proposing them. The crucial question is: are they worth what they cost? For years Congress—and state legislatures too—have never tried to analyze this question seriously. The prevailing philosophy has been, if it has a worthy objective, let's do it. As a nation, we're rich enough to afford it.

That simply isn't true any longer. That's what the persistent inflation should be telling us. The benefits we don't pay for through taxation, we are paying for through higher prices and a decrease in the value of our money. This inflation sometimes costs us more than 10¢ a year of every dollar we earn or own.

We can't hope to stop inflation until people begin to realize that government costs money. Not merely government programs that pay benefits, but all kinds of laws and government activities including those that regulate people and business. Laws cost the government money to interpret, administer, to enforce. They cost businesses additional billions just to comply—costs which have to be passed along to the consumer in higher prices. If it costs General Motors $600 to make the car you buy comply with government safety regulations, that car is going to cost you $600 more than it would have otherwise. If it costs the steel industry $100 million a year to eliminate pollutants from the smoke that pours out of its stacks, then steel will cost consumers $100 million more per year. Businesses have no secret source of funds. Every dollar they pay out—whether it's expenses, wages, or taxes—they have to get from their customers. That means you and me.

For generations, Americans have had the idea that if anything wasn't to their liking "there ought to be a law" to correct it. They've also had the notion,

somehow or other, that government was free. Nothing could be further from the truth. We pay for every move the government makes—and every costly move it forces industry to make. We pay for it through direct taxes and an amazing load of hidden taxes most people aren't even conscious of. We also pay for it through higher prices caused by inflation.

I don't mean to imply that these or other government programs don't have worthwhile objectives. But now is the time, if ever, to take a look at every government activity, old or new, and ask one simple question: is it really worth what it costs? If it is, let's do it. If it isn't, let's stop it. Let's definitely stop doing anything we're not willing to pay for in taxes. Otherwise inflation will keep rolling along.

Unfortunately, the belief still persists that the Federal Reserve Board can, or should be able to, stop inflation. It can momentarily, but only by policies which are so disastrous for the country that the cure is worse than the disease. The Federal Reserve, by refusing to create the money and credit the Government needs to borrow could throw the Federal Government into virtual bankruptcy. This is exactly what the Federal Reserve did to thousands of private businesses in its efforts to cool down inflation. It forced interest rates so high the businesses couldn't borrow the money they need to operate with.

The Federal Reserve's cure for inflation is suicidal. And it always has been, despite the popular fiction that the Federal Reserve should control inflation and deflation through the money supply. It can't. There is no practical way as long as the Government continues to run huge deficits.

The present inflation is devastating our society. Federal Reserve actions to tighten credit may stop it momentarily, but if the Federal Government keeps on running huge deficits, inflation will be back as bad or worse than ever.

Poor people, and older people on fixed incomes, are finding it more and more difficult to meet their bills. Thrifty people who have saved all their lives for a happy, independent old age are finding their savings worth less and less.

Colleges, universities, and hospitals, many of which rely on income from endowments to meet expenses are having more and more difficulty paying their bills. Their problems will probably get worse.

Public schools used to be supported without question. Now the burden of other spending and other taxes is so great schools are having difficulty getting the money they need. That too may get worse.

This is the price we pay for supposedly harmless Government deficits.

Suppose we stopped the Government deficits which contribute so heavily to inflation? What chance do we have of controlling the other important factor which makes prices go up, the big wage increases?

Stopping wage increases which exceed the gains in productivity wouldn't be hard to do if the public understood the problem. That's the real trouble. Most people still don't understand that these wage increases don't come out of employers' profits. If they did, profits—and the businesses—would soon disappear. Wage increases which exceed any increase in productivity *have* to be passed along to consumers by charging higher prices.

When people finally understand this, strikes by unions whose members are already among the highest paid in the country will no longer be visualized as labor versus capital, or the working man against the boss. Such strikes will be seen for exactly what they are—an attempt by employees who are already much better off than the average worker to gain further advantages.

These wage increases, with their disastrous effect on prices, can be stopped anytime a majority of people understand the situation and insist that they ought to be stopped.

Some Facts About Taxation

BEFORE EXPECTING the various governments, Federal, state, and local, to take on any more functions, or provide any more benefits, it might be wise to know what these governments are already costing us. Actually, Peter, this has been one of the best kept secrets in the country. The taxes we pay consciously and directly are only part of the load. In addition, there are hidden taxes included in the prices of everything we buy.

The most obvious burden is personal income taxes. Most of us are well aware of paying those. We also realize that some pretty substantial Social Security taxes are deducted from our pay. People who own their own homes are also conscious of the fact that they have to pay property taxes.

But what about the taxes and government charges we don't stop to think about—sales taxes and the taxes that are paid by the businesses whose products we buy? These hidden taxes, which are passed along to us in the prices we pay, actually amount to more than our income taxes, property taxes, and Social Security taxes all put together! The hidden tax burden is even bigger than the obvious one.

What do these hidden taxes consist of? All sorts of taxes paid by the businesses that supply the goods and services we use. Things like corporate property taxes, corporate income taxes, customs duties, general sales and gross receipts taxes, gasoline, liquor and tobacco taxes, motor vehicle licenses, public utility charges, and a hundred other taxes of one kind or another.

How do these taxes get passed along to us? Here's exactly how it happens. Let's assume, Peter, that you and I think we can make money manufacturing and selling XYZ gadgets. I've got $100,000 in a savings bank on which I am getting 5% interest. You tell me if I take a chance and go into business with you, I can make 20% on the money. I know it's risky, but that sounds like a pretty good return so I decide to take a chance.

Let's assume we're lucky. You were right—we do make a 20% return, $20,000 profit per year after income taxes.

But wait a minute! Suddenly the government doubles the income tax rate on small businesses. And the state adds a new processing tax on gadgets. Before you know it, our profit has been cut back to $5,000 a year after taxes.

That isn't enough return for the risk involved. I could get that much income, and my money would be a lot safer, back in the savings bank. Fortunately, however, all our competitors in the XYZ gadget business have been affected the same way. All of us are paying higher taxes and making too little return. Everybody is in the same boat, so we can all raise our prices without losing business to a competitor. So, one after another, we all raise our prices enough to get back the cost of the new taxes. The tax, in effect, is passed along to our customers.

Nobody has a right to force us to stay in the gadget business. And if we can't make a reasonable profit, we're not going to. Neither is anyone else. If customers still want XYZ gadgets, they'll have to pay a price high enough to cover the new taxes.

There's no conspiracy about this. And it's not a matter of tax evasion by business. It's simply an economic fact. Nobody starts a business for the fun of it. People start businesses because they hope to make a profit. If they don't make a reasonable profit, they fold up and quit as soon as possible.

In order to make a profit, a businessman has to charge the customer enough to cover *all* his expenses, and still have at least a little left over. That's his profit. When you increase his taxes, they are no different from any other business expense. He has to raise his prices enough to cover them. So the taxes get passed along to the customer, just like wage increases. There is no other way he can stay in business.

Some economists, Peter, agree that most business taxes are passed along to customers, but not the taxes on business income. They say the business income tax, which is figured on the final results, really comes out of the business. As a practicing businessman, I don't agree. The prices businesses charge are aimed at making a fair return *after all taxes*. I don't care what the income of my business is *before* income taxes. It's income *after* taxes that really matters. That's the return on my investment. If it isn't big enough to be worthwhile, I'll be raising prices every chance I get. The higher the taxes on business become, the higher the prices a businessman has to charge in order to wind up with a reasonable profit.

Don't assume from this that business people don't pay any taxes. They pay taxes on their personal incomes the same as anybody else. But taxes on the businesses they operate are passed along to the customers in higher prices whenever possible. In most cases it's not a matter of choice; it's a matter of survival.

There's no way of ducking the hidden taxes included in the cost of the things we buy, nor the sales taxes which are added to the price. Everyone, rich or poor, has to pay them in proportion to the amount of money he or she spends. At the present moment they take close to 20 cents of every dollar we buy things with.

Politicians prefer to tax businesses rather than individuals whenever possible. The obvious reason is that when a tax is hidden or included in the cost of things people buy, they are rarely aware of it. And what you don't see, you don't resent. On the other hand, when you raise the personal income tax or property tax rates, everybody is immediately alerted to the increased cost of government.

As this book is written, Peter, Government spending and the tax load seem almost out of control. In 1980, according to estimates of the Tax Foundation, the Federal, state, and local governments collected $3,286 in taxes for each man, woman, and child in the country. Twenty years earlier, in 1960, tax collections were $709 per person. In 1940, they were only $108 per person.

Part of this increase is due to inflation—but not the major part. Most of it represents a tremendous growth in government activities. The government is offering a great many services and benefits it didn't used to. There seems to be no limit to the public assistance the people of this country want. Old benefit programs seem to grow, year by year, in spite of efforts to control them. And new ones are still being added.

Medicare, medicaid, welfare, unemployment compensation, retirement pensions. Are these programs really worth what they cost us? Can we afford them without disastrous inflation? Are there cheaper and better ways to attain the same goals? Are they using up funds which would otherwise be available to improve the efficiency of industry and raise our standard of living? Are we so interested in welfare programs that we may cut defense spending to the point where we cannot adequately protect ourselves? I do not know the answers to these questions, Peter. I'm afraid they are problems for your generation. They may prove crucial to your future well being.

As long as we're talking about taxes, there's one more item we ought to cover. That's the idea that the rich really don't pay much in taxes, that most of their income is tax exempt. This is a popular rumor in some circles, but it doesn't jibe with the facts.

In the most recent year for which I have the final government figures, 90,000,000 people filed Federal Income Tax returns. Only 2% of these taxpayers—two out of every hundred—had adjusted gross incomes of $50,000 or more. Ninety-eight out of every hundred earned less than $50,000.

All together, the people who earned $50,000 or more got 12.2% of the total income. At the same time, however, they paid 25.6% of the total taxes. 2% of the people got 12.2% of the income and paid 25.6% of the taxes—that doesn't sound exactly like getting off scot-free, does it?

People with big incomes *do* pay taxes. Most of them pay a far larger portion of their incomes in taxes than people with smaller incomes. Yes, if they—or anyone—

want to risk lending their savings to states, counties, or cities, the interest they earn will be tax-free. The value of such investments, however, does *not* increase during inflation and they can, at times, be very risky. Incidentally, tax-free interest was not established with the idea of helping rich investors, but to help states and municipalities borrow money at a lower rate of interest.

There are also some industries the government wants to encourage—like oil exploration and low-priced housing—where companies get a special tax break. These tax advantages help offset some of the risk. They were granted to encourage certain special investments that would help the whole country. They are so misunderstood, however, that we might all be better off if they were phased out. At least it would help allay the idea that some people aren't carrying a fair share of the tax load.

We Have Only What We Produce

IN THIS WORLD, and in this country, we have to take care
of ourselves. No one else is going to do it for us. We've
got to grow or produce the things we need and want.
Either that, or grow and produce some things we can
trade with other countries in order to get what we
want. No one is going to give us a living. As a nation,
we're on our own. We have only what we produce.
That's what our standard of living depends on.

If our nation consisted of only a half-dozen people
who lived together on an isolated farm, with no
contact with the rest of the world, this would be
obvious. All of us would plainly see that if we wanted
something we would have to grow it or make it. And
the more we produced, the more we would have.

Actually, of course, our country consists of millions
of families. We work in hundreds of different industries and some of us live more than a thousand
miles away from each other. Yet the same basic fact is
true: we have *only* what we produce. That's what
limits and determines our overall standard of living.

In view of this, you'd expect that most of us would be
trying to produce *more* rather than *less*. Unfortunately, that's not true. We have become so confused by
arguments over who should get how much for doing
what that we have lost sight of the overall picture.

Many workers, over the years, have cut back, not only the time they will work, but how hard they are willing to work. Most of us want more and more money for doing less and less.

The fundamental tactic of organized labor has been to try to grab a bigger and bigger piece of the pie, each union concerned only about its own particular members. They think they've been getting this larger share out of profits which would otherwise go to the owners of the business. But, as we've pointed out before, they haven't been getting their wage increases out of profits. Profits are still taking about 5 cents out of every sales dollar just like they always have. Actually, workers have been getting these wage increases out of each other. We're all paying higher prices because of them.

While everybody has been grabbing for a larger share of the pie, nobody seems to be paying much attention to the size of the pie itself. The best way to increase the size of everybody's share is to produce a bigger pie! If we produce more and grow more, we'll all have more. If we don't, we won't.

This is so obvious—how can we possibly have ignored it?

One reason is that our shorter hours and slackening of individual effort have been more than offset by better methods, better tools and more productive machinery. The same force that made possible the tremendous advance in our standard of living in the last 200 years is still working. We're still investing money in new equipment that enables us to produce more and more with less time and effort.

Unfortunately, however, the rate of increase in our productivity—our output per man-hour of work—has slowed down alarmingly. According to estimates by the Department of Labor our production per man-hour increased 29% in the ten years between 1950 and 1960.

In the next decade, from 1960 to 1970, we kept booming along at almost the same rate. Productivity rose another 32%.

In the most recent ten years, however, from 1970 to 1980, the gain in production per man-hour slumped to 15%. Since 1977 we've been stumbling along, showing no gain whatever—in fact a tiny loss each year.

What's wrong?

Has the Government been borrowing and spending so much of the available capital that industry can't raise the amount it formerly did to spend for new and better equipment?

Have we forced industry to spend so much to improve the environment—by eliminating waste, smoke and noise—that it hasn't had enough left to improve productivity as much as it used to?

Have labor unions been resisting the introduction of more productive equipment and better methods for fear of losing jobs?

Have people been unable to save and invest as much as they used to because of taxes and inflation?

Have high taxes discouraged people from investing as much in industry as they used to?

It may be any one of these things, Peter—perhaps a little bit of all of them. I don't know for sure. But your generation had better dig in and find out *why* productivity isn't increasing the way it used to. If you don't, your future may be no better than our past, perhaps not as good.

You will have only what you produce. And what you produce will depend on how long and how efficiently you work.

What would happen, for example, if we all worked harder every day, and did our very best? Would it simply mean that all businesses would make larger profits? Only momentarily. Competition between producers would very shortly cause the savings from increased productivity to be passed along in lower prices. Competition would keep profits right about where they are now and we would all benefit from lower prices.

Some people can't believe that anything like this

could possibly happen. Yet competition between producers is real and continuous. That's why increased productivity and lower costs, sooner or later, benefit the consumer.

As a current television program says: "You've got to see it to believe it." Until you actually try to make and sell something yourself, it's hard to appreciate how much competition there really is and how much it helps the consumer.

Consider, for example, the introduction of the sewing machine. Before Singer invented it, most ordinary people couldn't afford new, factory-made clothes. They wore secondhand clothes and homespun instead. Singer's machine, however, made new, factory-made clothes so cheap almost everyone could afford them. Competition between clothing producers forced the benefits of the new machine to be passed along to everyone in the form of lower prices. We could produce more so we all had more.

But what happens to the workers when we introduce laborsaving machinery, for example, equipment that enables five workers to produce as many widgets as ten did before? Doesn't that mean that five workers lose their jobs? Not necessarily. The reduction in price made possible by the new machinery may increase demand for widgets so much nobody will be fired. We may need even more widget workers.

But what if demand is "inelastic"? What if the lower price doesn't increase the demand for widgets at all? Yes, then five widget workers will have lost their jobs because of the new machinery. But what about the money the customers save because widgets are now less expensive? Won't they spend that on something else? Of course they will! Most of us, despite the fears that there are only so many jobs in this world, have an endless list of wants. What we don't spend on widgets, we'll now spend on gadgets. The five former widget workers will have to shift over to making gadgets.

That's a hardship, yes. And those who have to shift and find new jobs should be publicly helped and compensated. But it's a necessary price we pay for progress. If we never introduced new laborsaving machinery, and nobody ever had to change jobs, we'd never be any better off than we are today. There would be no more increases in productivity or our standard of living.

What happens when people produce less? They all have less. An unusual example of this is two European automobile factories built by the Ford Motor Company to produce the Ford Escort. The factories were virtually identical, one in Halewood, England, the other in Saarlouis, West Germany.

The British workers and their union simply refused to use certain equipment and methods. As a result, it took 40 hours of labor to assemble an Escort car in the factory in England. In Germany, more quality-conscious, cooperative workers did the same job in 21 hours. Because of greater productivity, it was possible to pay the German workers $13.50 per hour. The British workers got only $8.25 per hour. Yet the cars made in Germany were still cheaper than those made in England. Naturally, Ford gave the German plant most of the business.

How could the British workers and unions expect to get more by producing less? Probably they expected to do it simply by demanding and grabbing a share of what they thought must be an exorbitant profit. But profits aren't that big. As we've mentioned before, in most companies they are only one-sixth to one-seventh as big as the compensation of employees. And profits can't be used to increase wages without destroying the business involved. Without profits there is no capital, no machinery, no tools, no reason for being in business.

More Production, Not Less

To HELP THE poor and the needy—and to make a satisfying life for all those who would like to do better—we need more production, not less.

One of the great illusions of this age—especially appealing to reformers everywhere—is that production is no longer a problem. We already grow enough and produce enough—so they say—to take care of all our needs. The trouble is, it's so poorly divided. The rich take too much and the poor get too little. If we divided everything up evenly, they claim, there'd be plenty for everyone.

It's an interesting theory, but doesn't hold water. Actually, there aren't enough rich people to consume—to literally use up—enough of our national product to make much difference. Individually, rich people undoubtedly eat more food—or at least waste more food—than poorer people do. They own a lot more clothes, but don't necessarily wear out a lot more because their old clothes are passed along to others. So are their automobiles, houses, stereos, and what have you. They own everything they can possibly need or want. But there's a definite limit to the amount one human being can use up or destroy. And what the rich don't use or destroy is generally salvaged and used by others.

The *excess* amount of food, clothing, and all other

worldly goods the rich actually *consume*—beyond
and above that consumed by the average person—is, I
suspect, comparatively unimportant. If we took all of
this excess consumption away, and gave it to the poor,
few people would notice much difference. It would
never eliminate poverty or need in a manner we would
like to see them eliminated.

If, as some believe, we already have an excess
production of goods, more than enough to meet the
needs and desires of everyone, where is it? Yes, we
occasionally have a bumper crop of corn or wheat that
sits in warehouses for a year or two. But that's just
about all. Even in good times, when most industries
are running close to capacity, goods are not piling up
in the warehouses. We use just about all the goods we
can produce, either to consume ourselves or to trade
with others. Yet there are still millions of people who
are poor and needy, and tens of millions more who
don't have as high a standard of living as they would
like.

As long as we are not using up irreplaceable natural
resources, why should we deny these people the right
to earn more and have more?

The only possible way to achieve this is by producing more goods, more efficiently. We can't do it
simply by taxing the rich to pay for bigger benefits to
the poor. If taxes eliminate too much of the savings
created by larger incomes—as some economists

believe they are doing right now—where will the money to provide new jobs come from? At present it takes an investment of more than $60,000 to provide the buildings, tools, equipment, and working capital required for a single worker in a manufacturing job.

The most significant difference between people with larger incomes and the average person is not in the amount they consume. It's in the amount they save. We rely on the savings of people with larger incomes to maintain and increase our production. People who save money and invest it help buy the tools and equipment that benefit all of us.

During the 20-year period from 1960 to 1980, the United States and Great Britain each put about 18% of their gross national product into new fixed capital in the private and government sectors of their economies. As a result, they both enjoyed an increase of more than 75% in productivity. Japan, during those same 20 years, put 33% of its gross national product into new fixed capital. Its productivity jumped more than 300%! Why the bigger jump? One obvious reason is that they invested far more in better production facilities.

Any economy constantly needs additional capital if it wants to produce more and have more. Under free enterprise these funds come voluntarily from private savings and investment. When incomes are so severely taxed that personal savings decline—or don't increase as fast as they used to—the increase in productivity slows down, perhaps stops. We produce less and we have less.

The age of irreversible plenty is not yet here. We cannot afford to give everyone every benefit the mind of man can imagine. Our economy is not that productive. By assuming that it is, we could seriously damage it—perhaps beyond repair.

The Importance Of Competition

THE FREE-ENTERPRISE system depends on competition. That's what makes it efficient and effective. Without it, the system simply doesn't work—at least not the way it should.

Competition for the consumer's dollar determines what we produce. If the consumer is willing to pay enough for widgets to more than cover the cost of making them, we produce widgets. If he won't, we don't. If he'll pay more for something else, we make that instead. No planning authority is required to make this happen; the consumer calls the tune and the market takes care of it automatically.

If some companies can produce widgets better and more cheaply than others, competition channels the business to them first. Competition, reflecting the will of the consumer, encourages those who do things better and cheaper.

And what about profits? If it weren't for competition, wouldn't many producers charge more for their output and make bigger profits? They certainly would. In fact, this is the root of a damaging criticism of the free-enterprise system. Many critics have insisted that there isn't enough competition under free enterprise. The lack of competition, they say, has resulted in monopolies which exploit the consumer and make exorbitant profits.

Is it true or isn't it? Frankly, Peter, I've known hundreds of people who believed it. On the other hand, I don't know a single soul who has tried to prove it, factually and statistically. I honestly doubt that anyone could. As a professional statistician and business editor, I have never run across any evidence which substantiates the charge that U.S. industries have increased their profits by monopolistic tactics.

Yes, there have been monopolies and cartels—often with government approval—in a number of foreign countries. But the United States happens to have antitrust laws which carry very severe penalties. Furthermore, in this country, profits for all companies of any appreciable size are a matter of public record. Not only that, but they have to be vouched for by certified public accountants.

In other words, if there were any "monopoly"

profits, they would have to be a matter of public record. But where are they? I have never observed nor heard of any group of companies which made abnormally large profits—profits big enough to support a suspicion of monopoly—for any appreciable length of time.

Admittedly, there are occasions, in local areas, when a few suppliers may manage to corner a market between them, divide up the available business, and charge higher prices. This usually happens in industries which are heavily unionized. The unions cooperate to prevent other competitors from entering the area. In return, union members get higher wages and some union leaders may get a few extras under the table. But there has never been any combine on a national scale big enough and successful enough to produce monopolistic profits for any one industry, and to keep on doing it year after year. Why not? I believe the antitrust laws have been far more effective than critics realize.

There are outstanding companies, yes, companies which make more money than others in their field. But they do it legally, by outstanding performance that pleases the consumer. They don't do it by collusion or illegal tactics. If they try to, competitors are the first to blow the whistle and have the Justice Department on their necks. But there's nothing illegal about doing a better job than the next fellow. Some well-managed organizations do it year after year.

Most of the price agreements discovered and prosecuted by the Government have NOT been agreements to *raise* prices. They have been agreements— made when demand began to soften—*not to cut* prices in order to steal each other's customers. They were *not* agreements designed to make the largest possible profit in good times, but to avoid cutthroat competition in bad times.

The Government itself tried to encourage agreements like this to speed recovery from the depression of the thirties. The Supreme Court, however, ruled such agreements illegal, and businessmen, generally, have found them distinctly unprofitable. Too many employees invariably know about such deals. Sooner or later, some disaffected party tips off the Justice Department. When the Government sues, the fines may run into hundreds of millions of dollars.

Price-fixing is *not* a major force in our economy. It's a minor blemish. If it were more than that, business profits would show it. They'd be a lot bigger than they are. It simply doesn't pay to violate the antitrust laws. Even if a company or group of companies get away with it for a while, the eventual penalties will more than wipe out any possible gains.

Despite this, a great many people still talk about monopolies and monopoly profits as if they were an everyday occurrence. So why not take a look at corporate profits and see if we can find some?

Whenever it is reported that a big company has made a profit totaling hundreds of millions of dollars, some people automatically hit the ceiling. It's unconscionable! How can any company make that much profit when some people are hungry and don't have good homes to live in?

Unfortunately, they don't stop to consider that this is the age of big enterprises. Some of the organizations we've developed to satisfy our needs are colossal. They have hundreds of thousands of employees. Hundreds of thousands of stockholders have invested billions of dollars to provide their buildings, equipment, and working capital. When you compare their earnings to the amount invested, you'll find that none of these big organizations is making an exorbitant return on its investment. Some of them aren't doing as well as the operator of your local candy store.

The fairest way to measure earnings is to compare them as a percentage return on the amount invested. When you deposit money in a savings bank, for example, you expect a return of about 5% a year. For every year you leave $100 in the bank, they will credit you with $5 interest. The return on your investment is 5%.

People who invest in common stocks are looking for a return on their investment too. The return on investment means how much is earned on the amount stockholders have invested in the business.

Another word for the stockholders' investment in a company is *net worth*. If you take the total assets—everything a business owns—and subtract all of its liabilities—everything it owes—what's left is the net worth. The net worth is what belongs, free and clear, to the stockholders. Return on investment or return on net worth are two ways of saying the same thing.

For all active corporations in the United States, the return on investment in the last ten years has averaged less than 10%. For manufacturing companies it has been running somewhere between 11% and 16%.

Investors don't actually receive this much in dividends. For years it has been customary for companies to keep more than half of the profits they earn and reinvest them in the business. During the 1970's, because of inflation, and the need to replace inventories and equipment at higher prices, companies retained almost two-thirds of their earnings. The rest, slightly more than one-third of the profits, was paid out in dividends to stockholders. Retained earnings, of course, help a company grow and make it stronger. If successfully reinvested, they will help produce larger profits in the future.

Are these profits shockingly large? I suspect that most people would be shocked to learn they are so small. Few things have been so exaggerated by the media as the relative size of business profits. Actually, at the present moment (early 1982), interest rates are so high, you can make a bigger return by putting your money into minimum risk money funds or high-grade bonds.

Despite this, there are still more than 27 million people in the United States who own stock in business corporations. They hope, eventually, to make a higher return—at least higher compared to the interest on bonds, savings accounts, and so-called "safe" investments. Interestingly enough, all these stockholders aren't wealthy. More than 11 million of them had annual incomes of less than $25,000 in 1980. Industry has lots of small owners as well as big ones.

In order for a company to make 20% or more on its capital, it has to be extremely well-situated—a leading company in a growing field—and extremely well managed. A huge reference volume on my desk, the Value Line Investment Service, reports the operating results of more than 1,700 leading companies. On one page it lists the companies which have had an average return of more than 20% on their investment for the last five years. Only 90 out of the 1,700 companies—only about one company out of every twenty—was that profitable.

If it takes collusion to produce bigger profits, you can't prove it from this list. No industry is prominent on the list. Very few of the most profitable companies are even in the same business. The unusually profitable companies represent a wide range of businesses: real estate, retailing, auto & truck, health care, insurance, electrical equipment, aerospace, publishing, telecommunications, office equipment, computers, oil field services, food processing, petroleum, industrial services, electronics, building, precision instruments, metal fabricating, machinery, etc., etc., etc.

The way these companies make bigger than average profits is not by conniving or making price agreements with competitors. Neither is it by using illegal tactics to drive competitors out of the business. It is by moving into fast growing fields—where demand is so strong and production still so inadequate that it makes possible very good prices. This is a situation that doesn't last forever—competition is invariably attracted to profitable industries and eventually catches up. Then the rate of return goes down.

That's the reason so many companies are constantly looking for new fields—fast growing ones. That's where the profit is better. The annual report of one company, which recently crossed my desk, shows they have made an average of more than 30% on their invested capital for the last five years! They are not a huge outfit, just a moderate size company, but they have gotten into five different, fast growing industries and have found themselves an excellent niche in each of them.

What about the so-called "oil monopoly", the Seven Sisters, the seven big oil companies who are supposedly getting rich at the expense of all the rest of us? In the last three years Mobil Corp. has had an average return on investment of 19%. Exxon averaged a shade over 20%. But let's give them credit—they are both excellently managed companies, well-situated in an industry with a tremendous growth record.

The absolute size of their profit figures is stunning. But when you put them into perspective—compare them to the investment—it's a different picture. Last year Mobil Corp., for example, had a net profit of more than two billion, four hundred million dollars. Colossal! But they also had more than 200,000 employees and almost 300,000 stockholders. These stockholders have invested more than fifteen billion dollars to develop a worldwide petroleum business.

One of the interesting things about the Seven Sisters, Peter, is that they are *all* publicly-owned companies with hundreds of thousands of stock-holders. Anyone who wants to can share in the ownership. A stockbroker will be delighted to sell you shares in any one of them. Then you can be an insider instead of an outsider. The Securities and Exchange Commission, furthermore, will see that you are treated exactly the same as every other stockholder.

The morning I am writing this, for example, you could buy a share of Exxon for $29 and it is currently paying a dividend of $3 a year. That's an annual yield of more than 10% a year. At that price, how come people aren't falling all over themselves to buy it? Because the future of the international oil business seems very uncertain right now. And if profits do go up, what certainty is there that a revenue-hungry U.S. government will let the oil industry keep them? Being in the oil business these days is not exactly the picnic it has been painted.

More About Monopoly

I CAN STILL remember the hullabaloo speakers and writers used to make about the steel "monopoly" twenty or thirty years ago. We don't hear much about that anymore. Maybe it's because U.S. Steel made only 4.6% on its invested capital in 1978, had a deficit in 1979, and made only 8.7% in 1980. I wonder, Peter, what happened to the so-called "monopoly"?

Nobody likes the idea of monopoly. What it represents, basically, is a small group of people conniving and using unfair tactics to take advantage of the rest of us. That's probably why monopoly charges are always so sensationalized. It comes under the old-fashioned heading of a "dastardly deed".

The tactics supposedly used, or actually used, by monopolists have been highly publicized: price cutting in order to force some competitors out of business, buying up others, and forcing big rebates from suppliers, rebates smaller competitors can't hope to get. But if these tactics are so widespread and so successful, then where are the monopolies and monopoly profits they were supposed to create? I see no evidence of them, Peter. That's why I feel the whole issue, at least today, is greatly exaggerated. Either U.S. industry is far more competitive than most critics realize, or the antitrust laws have been amazingly efficient. The right answer, I believe, includes a bit of both.

One trouble is that tactics which may be called "monopolistic" by competitors are the same tactics which a successful concern sometimes adopts to give better value to customers and solidify its position in the market. So how do you tell which is which? How much competition is desirable and fair, and at what point does it become monopolistic?

One of the most fascinating monopoly cases is the one which involved John D. Rockefeller and the Standard Oil Company of New Jersey. In 1870, when Rockefeller formed the company it had only 4 percent of the total refining capacity in the country. Thirty years later, in 1900, it had 90 percent.

A monopoly? For all practical purposes, yes. But as far as the consumer was concerned, it didn't act like one. During those same 30 years, Rockefeller's company reduced the price of kerosene from 26 cents a gallon to 6 cents a gallon! The Standard Oil Company pioneered the techniques of handling and refining petroleum from the well to the customer. Its methods were so efficient and so cost-cutting that many companies simply couldn't compete. They had to get out of the business.

By the turn of the century, however, competitors were beginning to smarten up. Copying Standard's methods, and developing better techniques of their own in new areas, they began cutting back Standard's share of the business. In 1911, nevertheless, the

Supreme Court ordered Standard Oil broken up into several different companies. The Court did not find, interestingly enough, that Standard Oil was guilty of employing anticompetitive practices. It simply ruled that competition between some divisions of Standard Oil was less than it used to be when they were separate companies. Therefore, said the Supreme Court, it should be broken up.

The Aluminum Company of America lost an anti-trust case too. Does this mean it was guilty of some heinous crime or conspiracy? No—the company was never convicted of doing anything against the public interest. It was simply too big—it owned in one company too much of the country's capacity for making aluminum. And, according to the way the Supreme Court interpreted the antitrust laws, that wasn't right.

That's one of the big troubles: what do the antitrust laws mean? Exactly what do they prohibit and what do they condone? Actually, nobody knows. It depends on how the Justice Department wants to interpret the laws at that moment, and whether or not a majority of the Supreme Court Justices happens to agree. And the fact they agree today does not guarantee that the same or new Justices will agree five or ten years from now.

When it's hard to determine what the law really means, and how it might be interpreted under current conditions, how can you be sure you're not violating it? And how can Government departments enforce it intelligently? I never realized what a problem this is until I read a recent book by Robert H. Bork, former U.S. Solicitor General and a Yale law professor. The title of his book is, "The Anti-Trust Paradox—A Policy at War with Itself." Anyone who thinks that antitrust is a simple matter of the good guys versus the bad guys should get hold of a copy and read it.

Most of the big antitrust suits these days are not about price-fixing. Nor has anyone necessarily committed a crime. The Government often sues to prevent mergers and acquisitions which it thinks might lessen competition. How? By concentrating production in any industry into what it considers "too few" competitors.

But how does the Government know—who in the Government is smart enough to know—how many competitors there ought to be in each line of business?

This is the age of MASS PRODUCTION. In many industries THE ECONOMIES OF SCALE force companies to produce in huge quantities in order to lower costs and compete in the market. Sometimes a market isn't big enough—there isn't enough demand for the product—to support more than two or three such producers. The fact that there are only a few companies in an industry doesn't necessarily reflect (as some people seem to believe) connivance, collusion, or dirty work at the crossroads. Neither does it mean there is no competition.

Big companies are not a crime—in many industries the economies of scale make them an absolute necessity. If the Government should insist, for example, that automobiles had to be produced by 25 different domestic companies instead of 3 or 4, they would cost us a lot more than they do today.

The most serious monopoly threat these days, from the consumer's point of view, comes from organized labor. By organizing all the producers in an industry—such as automobiles—and making it impossible for manufacturers to hire anyone else, a union can create a labor monopoly and force up the wage level. Such moves have cost American consumers more money than any business monopoly anyone ever dreamed of. In the automobile industry the union pushed its members' wages and benefits far above the national average. This forced up the price of domestic automobiles and we lost a big piece of the business to Japan.

Some people urge that we protect American automobile workers with a tariff that will make Japanese cars cost more. Others are more reluctant. If Japanese cars cost more, won't American cars cost more too?

This is a problem which our country, as a nation, has not yet faced up to. According to traditional thinking, the working man is holy. Therefore, we've established laws which force employers to deal with unions and exempt unions from antitrust prosecution. We've done this, supposedly, to help employees get more OUT OF their employers. But industry-wide wage increases DON'T come OUT OF employers. When *all* employers have to pay the same wage increase, everyone simply passes it along in *higher prices*. That's what has been happening year after year, and we still don't seem to realize it. Big wage increases for special groups don't help working people as a whole. They only help the groups that receive them. Everyone else has to pay for them in higher prices.

Where Capital Comes From

WHEN WE SPEAK of CAPITAL, we usually mean the money required to start a business and keep it going. CAPITAL GOODS are the things that capital is used to buy—things like buildings, machinery, and equipment. Sometimes we use the words more or less interchangeably.

A business can't operate without capital. Neither can a country. The more capital equipment a nation has, the more goods it can produce. And the more it produces, the more people have, and the higher the standard of living for everyone. Prices are lower and wages are higher.

If capital is so important, where does it come from, and how can we be sure of maintaining a good supply? That is not only a good question—it may well be the most significant question of our era.

The money to create and operate business enterprises comes, basically, from three sources, equity, debt, and trade credit. Let's forget about trade credit for the moment because that's relatively simple. It's the 30 day or 60 day credit which vendors of materials and supplies normally extend to a business. When they make a delivery to a sound, trustworthy customer, they don't demand cash. They get a receipt and leave a bill. Or their company mails a bill later. It's pretty routine, and that's all there is to trade credit, so let's not waste time with it. Equity and debt are the most important sources of capital to worry about. If you can't raise enough capital through equity and debt to pay your bills reliably, no one is going to extend you trade credit anyway.

The difference between equity and debt is simple and clear-cut. Equity money represents a share in the ownership and the profits and losses of the enterprise. Debt is a loan which bears a fixed rate of interest and has to be repaid, sometimes on demand, sometimes on a fixed date. It doesn't share in the profits or losses. If a company doesn't repay a loan on time, or fails to pay the interest, the lender can throw the company into bankruptcy, and often has a first claim on certain corporate assets—depending on the terms of the loan agreement. Loans may sometimes be available on more attractive terms than selling more stock, especially when interest rates are low. And if you make a large profit, you don't have to give the lender a larger share—simply pay the agreed rate of interest on his loan.

On the other hand, as many companies have been finding out to their dismay these last few years, debt can be dangerous. What if, during a recession, earnings sink so low that a company can't meet its interest payments? What if the debt comes due at a time when the company's credit standing isn't very good and it can't be repaid or renewed? What if a debt which bears a relatively low rate of interest comes due and has to be refinanced at a time when interest rates have soared to double or triple their previous level? What will the increased interest expense on the replacement debt do to the company's earnings? Thousands of companies that increased their debt financing during the recent inflation are facing these very problems right now, as I am writing this.

In corporations, equity is usually called by the name of common, or capital, stock. It is held mainly by individuals, and by some investment funds and pension funds which represent the combined savings of a great many people.

Preferred stock is another form of equity, but not too important in the overall picture. It gives the holder a prior claim to dividends—if and when dividends are paid—and a prior claim, ahead of the common stock-holder, if the company is dissolved. Preferred stock dividends, however, are usually at a fixed rate, and the preferred stockholder does *not* share in the gains if the company is a big winner. Those gains belong to the common stockholder. If a company fails to pay dividends, all a preferred stockholder can do is sit and wait and hope. Unlike a disappointed creditor, he can't throw the company into bankruptcy.

Debt is usually in the form of bank loans, loans from insurance companies, or publicly-financed debt in the form of bonds or debentures. These are usually sold to any investor who wants to buy them. Some people like to buy corporate bonds, just like others buy government bonds. The risk is greater but they pay higher interest than government bonds.

The difference between bonds and debentures is usually that bonded debt is backed by a mortgage. This gives the bondholders a lien on specific assets to which they have prior right in case the company defaults. Debentures are backed simply by the general credit of a company. They don't have a claim on any particular assets. In case of bankruptcy, the debenture holders are in the same boat as all the other creditors.

An individual or group starting a new business must usually depend, to begin with anyway, on equity capital. Somebody has to risk his personal or business savings to get the thing started. Very few people or institutions are interested in lending money to an entirely new enterprise. Why? Because they want to be paid back, and the moderate amount of interest they can receive, under our usury laws, can't possibly compensate for the tremendous risk. New businesses are far from a sure thing. Most of them fail within five years. Only a very small proportion turn into significant, consistent money-makers.

Anyone considering lending money to a business has to consider how it will be paid back. Normally there are two ways. One way is out of earnings. The other way is through a prior claim on company assets which can be sold for more than enough to cover the loan. New enterprises don't have *proven* earnings. And very few of them have assets which, if the business failed, could safely be sold for enough to repay a substantial loan. That's why it's very hard for new businesses to get credit. Credit usually comes only gradually, as businesses prove their ability to make money and meet their obligations.

If an individual's effort to start a new corporation fails, he can deduct the loss from other capital gains— if he has any. And there's the rub: many entrepreneurs don't have capital gains. They are risking everything on this one throw. If he doesn't have any capital gains, he can deduct only half the loss from his regular income, and at a rate of not more than $3,000 a year. In other words, if he has lost $60,000, it will take 10 years before he can deduct $30,000 from the income reported on his tax return. Not only the laws of chance, but our grasping tax laws are heavily weighted against the new entrepreneur. One might well ask, does this country want and need new businesses or doesn't it?

How Much Equity?
How Much Debt?

Every business has to decide for itself how much of its capital shall consist of equity, contributed by the owners, and how much should come from borrowing. Sometimes, Peter, it's not a matter of choice, but a matter of necessity. If an enterprise doesn't have a good enough credit rating to borrow money, it has to sell stock and take in more owners. And that isn't always easy.

If a company is in good financial condition, with a good earnings record, it may have a choice of borrowing or selling more stock. Which it does will depend on current conditions and company policy.

It is definitely riskier to use borrowed money than equity capital. There are excellent, conservative companies that, except for an occasional short-term bank loan, don't used borrowed money at all. The amount of risk, however, depends to a great extent on the nature of the business. If the business is long established and earnings are stable—if they don't flutter up and down with the business cycle—the likelihood of being unable to pay the interest, or repay or refinance the note when it comes due, is much less. Big public utility companies, for example, which have a guaranteed market, guaranteed rates, and no competition, often rely on borrowing for more than half their capital. Communities argue about utility rates, and may sometimes prevent a utility from charging enough to make a good return on its investment. They rarely, however, permit a utility to go broke. For that reason, it's much safer for a utility to borrow than it is for the ordinary competitive business.

Borrowing a reasonable amount of money isn't necessarily risky or inadvisable. But borrowing too much is. Smart management knows when, if it wants to be conservative, it should pull in its horns. There are many, many excellent companies that borrow up to 20% of their capital and no one thinks twice about it. If they start borrowing 35%, however, financial analysts begin to take notice. If the company eventually reaches the point where it is borrowing 50% or more of its capital, the people on Wall Street begin to watch the situation much more closely. The company is recognized as being a more risky investment than it used to be.

The company that raises capital through selling stock never has to worry about paying interest on it or paying it back. The company that borrows capital *does* have to worry about these things. Any day it can't meet the interest or repayment schedule, it may find itself in bankruptcy, with severe losses to all its stockholders.

These days the principal source of funds for modernization and expansion is internal, not external. Recently more than half of industry's new capital has come from inside sources—retained earnings and depreciation charges. Depreciation charges, so-called capital consumption allowances, are the amount industry is allowed to deduct from its earnings every year to pay for the estimated cost of plant, tools, and machinery used up or worn out during the period. For example, if a company pays $1,000,000 for some equipment that is expected to last about five years, it is allowed to deduct $200,000 a year from its earnings as depreciation. This amount is really not an increase in the company's capital. Together with retained profits, however, it does provide capital for replacing the worn-out equipment.

One of the problems is that, in this inflationary era, depreciation charges based on the former price of equipment are totally inadequate to replace it. The old equipment, which cost $1,000,000 five years ago, may now cost $2,000,000. Because the tax laws don't recognize this, many companies that appeared well off have found themselves desperately searching for new capital. They aren't doing nearly as well as their profits looked.

Most corporations have always reinvested a substantial portion of their earnings instead of paying them all out in dividends to stockholders. In the five years from 1976-80, business corporations actually retained twice as much as they paid out in dividends. This corporate thriftiness—or stinginess with stockholders—has been a major factor in keeping our gross private savings rate close to 20% of our national income. That's reasonably respectable, even though lower than most other industrialized countries. The thing that is way down is our rate of personal savings. In the last half of the 1970's we Americans saved less than 6% of our disposable personal income. Citizens of France, Germany, Italy, and Japan saved more than 14% of their income.

Recently our supply of new *equity* capital has consisted almost entirely of retained corporate earnings, not new personal savings. In the five years from 1976-80, corporations raised $644 billion of new money from outside sources. Of this amount only $31 billion was new equity. More than $600 billion was debt.

Obviously, debt capital has been increasing much faster than equity. In 1960, the capital and surplus (that's the total equity) of American corporations was equal to 34% of their total liabilities. By 1977, according to the Statistical Abstract, equity had dropped to 25% of total liabilities. In view of the pace at which U.S. industry has been borrowing money, equity has undoubtedly dropped even further since.

At the same time, the public interest in buying common stocks has declined sharply. In 1966, according to a Federal Reserve Board study, the financial assets of

American households were 39% invested in common stocks. By 1980 only 26% of the financial assets of American households were invested in common stocks.

The American public doesn't seem so anxious to take the risks of stock ownership anymore. It is lending more of its money now instead of risking it in equities. Deposits, mortgages, and bonds have jumped from 40% of total household assets to 50%. Pension fund reserves have risen from 11% to 16%.

I hesitate, Peter, to sound like an alarmist, but I wonder where the equity capital of the future will come from. Between the needs of industry and the growing needs of government, we may be facing a severe squeeze.

Recently, in addition to retained earnings, corporations have been using an average of more than $130 billion a year in new capital, almost all of it borrowed. Corporations, however, represent only about 75% of total business activity; the rest is done by farmers and unincorporated businesses. Unincorporated business, I would guess, may not use quite as much new capital. Their requirements, however, added to the corporate needs, might put industry's new capital needs over $150 billion per year.

Besides this, we have experienced a period of rapidly rising government deficits. The Federal Government will also be requiring more capital. A very conservative estimate would be $100 billion to $200 billion a year. Add this to corporate requirements and it makes a total need of perhaps $250 billion to $350 billion of new, outside capital every year.

Where is this kind of money going to come from? Not from personal savings. They hit a peak of $101 billion in 1980, less than 8% higher than the total five years earlier. That's obviously not enough to take care of the needs of both industry and government.

The obvious short-term answer, despite the equally obvious objections to it, is that both industry and the government will have to borrow more money. This new money will have to be created by the Federal Reserve and the banking system in the same way they created the new money that caused inflation in the past. That means more inflation. But if the Federal Reserve refuses to take care of this need, I simply can't imagine what will happen. Our welfare state will start wasting away for lack of capital.

There is at least one possible alternative. That is the proposal that President Reagan made and that so many critics assailed as economic nonsense. Cut government spending so the government uses less of our income, and eliminate the deficit. Also cut taxes so people have more money to invest.

Instead of complaining about the size of profits, maybe we'd better do something to make common stocks more attractive. According to the Federal Reserve Board, real profits, after allowing for inflation, have been averaging only 10% to 12% on the stockholder's investment. When interest rates are as high as they've been lately, you can get more than that on much safer investments, such as a money fund. Money funds invest in treasury bills, bank certificates of deposit, and commercial paper. In times of high interest rates they sometimes pay as high as 15%.

We need equity money. The longer we ignore that need, the more we are going to suffer from the overexpansion of debt and, eventually, an underexpansion in production and new jobs.

Some people will urge that the government become directly involved and supply equity money to companies that obviously need it. But how can the government do this without creating bigger deficits and more and worse inflation? And what safeguards would we have that government-supplied funds would be invested wisely and well? There's a tremendous difference between investing money the government gives or lends you, and putting your own savings on the line. That difference, I'm afraid, would show up immediately in more failures and soaring losses.

I suspect, Peter, that our industry can best be developed and run the same way it has been in the past—by people who have a personal financial stake in its success or failure. In order to have such people, we've got to let citizens who might be able to invest keep enough income to be able to do so. We may even find it necessary to provide additional incentives, such as some form of tax rebate, for new equity investments.

Problems, Problems

IT WOULD SEEM, Peter, that we have a few problems ahead of us.

We're not getting the productivity gains we used to. That means our standard of living is standing still— or soon will be—and may eventually begin to decline.

We've taxed ourselves so heavily—the bigger the income, the higher the rates—that we are no longer saving enough to expand production at the rate we used to.

Industry has been using debt instead of equity to increase its capital funds. That trend is unsound and can't continue indefinitely.

As a people, we have nurtured ambitions which are presently far beyond our abilities to fulfill. Workers want more and more money, sometimes for doing less and less. We've adopted social welfare, benefit, and security programs whose costs are increasing far beyond our ability to pay. Social benefits paid for by deficit financing are causing inflation which taxes everyone, the poor far more painfully than the rich.

The greatest problem of all is that so few people understand how and why this has happened. This is a democracy, and the voting majority, unenlightened though it may be, is still at the wheel. How long do you suppose it will take, Peter, before a majority of the people understand the changes that are necessary to make free enterprise work better for all of us? It may be a sheer impossibility. In that case, hadn't we better try something else? Like socialism, perhaps?

I wish I could consider this possibility seriously. But I can't—and perhaps that's unfair. You see socialism, the idea intellectuals talk about and admire, is exactly that—an idea. It has never really existed and been practiced by a free people on a national scale. A few socialist communities of people who share the same religion or social philosophy have lasted for some years. But there is nothing at all to indicate that the same idea would be possible—and produce as good results as free enterprise—on a national scale.

The communists have used socialism to organize their economies. Yet none of them has achieved a standard of living even close to that of the free nations. Perhaps this isn't a fair comparison, because the philosophy of communism was also involved. On the other hand, it definitely isn't encouraging.

Even those countries where people are openly dissatisfied with the profit system, and the socialist party has won control, have been loath to abandon a market system. The profit motive still dictates what shall be produced, and by whom. What could they possibly substitute in place of it? The attempts made to socialize various industries have not improved production or helped the nation. In most cases they have merely increased the national deficit. Since 1968 Great Britain has nationalized its steel industry, denationalized, then nationalized it again. Both the country and the industry are in pretty dismal shape, economically. The steel workers, however, seem securely positioned at the public trough.

Socialism—an economy managed and directed by the central government—is by no means totally ineffective. It can definitely achieve limited objectives—like building up a nation's armaments, or making medical services more widely available. But it simply isn't efficient enough, or flexible enough, to achieve the thousands of different objectives desired by millions of citizens.

That's the strength of private enterprise—it's a system developed over the years for producing what people really want—not what the government wants them to have—and doing it efficiently. Under private enterprise the most efficient producers get the business first. And bosses are picked by the results they produce. Under socialism, without profits, how do you measure efficiency and results? And who cares? Bosses are picked by vote or by influence, not by the test of competitive results.

I can't get too much concerned over the size of profits or who gets them. All I care is that they continue to be earned in a competitive market. If anyone is concerned about productive efficiency and a high standard of living—and quite frankly I am—the profit system has no rival. If it is even 10% more efficient than other systems, it's well worth what it costs—and more.

The crucial difference between profit-making organizations and government agencies lies in motivation. The private businessman usually has his own money at stake, as well as additional money from other stockholders who will be hollering for his scalp if he loses it. He is always faced with competition—not merely present competitors but potential new competitors who may step in anytime they think they can do the job better or cheaper.

The better a businessman is at controlling expenses, the bigger the profits and the bigger the rewards for management and workers. If he can't operate efficiently, can't control his expenses, the profits will dry up—and so will the business. Thousands of private businesses go broke every year—sometimes more than 10,000 in a single twelve-month period.

There's no way the private businessman can get careless, stop worrying about being efficient, and still be successful. Competition keeps his nose to the grindstone.

The motivation in a government agency is utterly different.

No one has a personal financial stake in a government operation. No one has to make a profit. Inefficiency and red tape are no skin off anyone's nose. They just create more jobs, necessitate bigger budgets, and make the manager's job seem more important.

In government, if costs go up, what difference does it make? There's no competition, no one to show how inefficient you are, no one to put you out of business by doing it better. And it's only the taxpayers' money anyway, so why fret?

If someone thinks of a way to cut expenses, that's interesting—but let's not be in too much of a hurry. If a government agency gets so efficient it cuts down the number of people it uses, it may, by the same act, reduce the relative importance of the manager's job, even his salary. Government agencies are *not*, by their very nature, an environment that encourages or demands cost-cutting and efficiency.

For the benefit of everyone, we *must* have a productive economy. Our standard of living depends on it. If, in order to achieve it, we have to let some people make more money than others, so be it! We are all better off as a result, including the poorest and lowest paid. Greater production, stimulated by personal rewards and incentives, means more goods and cheaper goods for everyone.

Suggestions that we adopt socialism as our national economic system always remind me of a quote from James Lincoln. James Lincoln was a tremendously successful executive who built the Lincoln Electric Company. He paid workers extremely generously, developing many types of incentive pay. What he said, Peter, and I suggest you take a little time to think about it, was as follows: "If we do not face up to the reward of winning and the penalty of losing, we will upset the whole system on which the progress of the human race is based." Amen.

So What Can We Do?

I SUSPECT, PETER, that if you prefer the personal freedom and initiative of private enterprise, as I do, the next decade will find you pretty much on the defensive. I'm afraid the best you can expect is to keep people and the government from damaging the private enterprise system any more than you can help. Eventually, if we can keep the profit system in existence—and the people trying to promote socialism here and elsewhere keep finding that it doesn't work too well—the tide may turn. One of the most encouraging signs is how many communist countries are quietly sneaking back to the free market system for at least part of their economies. Why? Because it gives people more incentive and obviously works better.

But don't expect results too soon. The people of this country are still emotionally fired up by the idea that PROFITS ARE TOO BIG. It will take a lot of time before that idea can be dislodged.

Another thing we should try to do is to try to dispel the idea that any economic system—free enterprise, socialism, or what have you—can possibly be perfect. There will always be defects in any system we adopt. Therefore, wouldn't it be smarter to try to patch up some of the defects in free enterprise, a system that has done so much for this country, rather than to buy one that is relatively untried, and has a totally unimpressive record of results?

Some of the things people don't like about free enterprise can be patched up or made allowance for. Others can't. The danger is that in passing laws to try to change one thing, we may put something else out of order. The minimum wage law, for example, was supposed to improve the income of lower paid workers. But you can't force people to pay more than they believe something is worth. The result of the law was to eliminate thousands of jobs—people preferred to do without a product or service rather than overpay. The law cut down the jobs available for inexperienced novices and seriously increased teenage unemployment.

Business cycles are something the government thinks it should be able to cure. It has been trying to eliminate them ever since the days of Franklin D. Roosevelt. I don't think it can be done. As long as people are free to do what they please, a lot of them are going to get overoptimistic and overexpand at the same time. That helps make a boom. When they all have to retract somewhat, that makes a bust—or at least a recession.

In the last 50 years, the average business cycle has lasted four years, three years up, then one year down.

The normal recession happens so unexpectedly, and is over so soon, that there's not much Congress can do about it. It takes too long to develop emergency employment programs and such things. By the time they are ready, the next upswing is underway. And what happens when you stop these emergency programs? A sudden break in the flow of funds may contribute to another recession.

I'm afraid the best thing the government can do about recessions is to stay out of the way and pick up the pieces. Have a good unemployment compensation program ready for emergencies and keep it going as long as necessary. But don't let's pretend we can stop the cycles, or even that we *ought* to be able to stop them. They are part of the price of letting people be free to do their own thing. Despite the cycles, we produce more and we have more under private enterprise than we possibly could under socialism.

Another thing people don't like about the profit system is the lack of job security. Under competitive conditions, you never can tell when somebody is going to develop a better product, or a better method, and put you out of business.

That's perfectly true, and a lot of people have suffered from it. But think of the numbers who have benefited from it! The better product or better method which causes some people to lose their jobs *helps* thousands of others.

This is the price we pay for progress. We shouldn't try to avoid change, but we should have a good unemployment and retraining program to cushion the pains. People who lose their jobs should be publicly helped, if they need it, to learn how to do something else and get a new job. But we can't just keep on producing the same old products in order to guarantee employment. If we did, we'd have warehouses full of corsets and one-horse shays. And people would still be making them.

Some people say free enterprise can't provide enough jobs—if we stick with it we'll always have unemployment. That's not true. The sizable unemployment we've had recently is not the fault of free enterprise. It's the responsibility of those who have been taxing away the savings free enterprise needs in order to expand. We still need more production. Many families would like more of a lot of things. More jobs will be available if and when we get the capital together to provide them. Until then, they won't be. We've got to stop killing the incentives for people to save money and the incentives to risk it in building businesses. And that's exactly what our welfare state has been doing.

True, we won't have executive jobs for everyone. The customer, under free enterprise, is still the boss. All we'll have are the jobs which are necessary to produce the things the customer wants.

The notion that we have to have a lot of government services in order to provide enough jobs for everyone simply doesn't hold water. Instead of taxing people to provide money for government jobs, why not let them keep the money and spend it for something else? Or invest it? Most families would be delighted to do so. The resulting demand would provide increased jobs—not make-work jobs but jobs making things people really need and want.

One of your toughest problems will be to stop the persistent increase in government spending before it entirely devours the savings and capital we need to produce goods. The difficulty is that the people of this country are actually more kind and generous than they can afford to be. They want to help everybody with a problem—regardless. As a result, the steadily increasing benefits we pay to special groups are so large they cause constant inflation for everyone else.

Benefit programs are difficult to control. Even if only 10% of the spending under a program is really justified, even if only 10% of the people who receive the benefits really need them, those 10% will be dramatized before Congress and the media. These cases will be used to mandate continuation of the whole program.

Somehow, Peter, we've got to face up to the fact that our Federal Government does *not* have a bottomless bucket of money. Congress—and the people pushing it for more benefits—have got to decide what benefits we want and need most, and what we can afford to pay for in taxes without seriously damaging the economy.

Also, Peter, we need a new philosophy of government benefits. Our aim should be, not just to *give* people things, but, wherever possible, to help people *earn* them. Is the only goal of our society people with well-fed, healthy bodies? Or is it also people of character and self-reliance? Nothing destroys character quicker than something for nothing. You know that, I know that, everybody knows that. So why don't we build our assistance programs as much as possible along other lines?

Something for nothing gets to be demoralizing and demeaning. What we need, if we can develop it, is a welfare and benefit philosophy of *something* for *something*. Any able-bodied person who accepts public benefits should be expected, whenever possible, to donate some of his or her time to perform public service—even if it's just picking up wastepaper and making this world a cleaner and neater place to live.

Every place this idea has been tried, it has immediately cut down the graft and unjustified claims. And there's not the slightest thing wrong with it. It's not demeaning. No work is demeaning if you do it with a whole heart and do it well.

The continuing Federal deficits are evidence, I'm afraid, that we, as a people, have been overreaching ourselves. It reminds me of a parable I heard in my childhood about a dog crossing a bridge over a stream. He had a huge bone between his jaws. As he looked down into the water, he suddenly saw his own image. Thinking it was another dog with a bigger bone, he snapped at it and lost his own bone in the water. I can't recall thinking of that story in fifty years, but there's something about the American people today that keeps bringing it to mind. What if, in snapping at a bigger bone, we lost the one we already have?

Well, that's all there is, Peter, for now anyway. If I searched around I might find another idea or two, but I wouldn't want you to accuse me of being long-winded. I'm afraid the rest of the job is up to you and your generation. Good Luck!

With love and best wishes,

Grandpa John

Afterthoughts

It's been four years since I wrote the earlier chapters in this book, Peter. You'll soon be going away to college. I wonder if I've omitted any ideas that might be helpful.

As far as I can see, the economic situation hasn't changed much. Some people seem to think inflation is behind us. They say the problem of rising prices has been licked.

I doubt that. We haven't stopped the government deficits yet. Once we hit a period of good business—a real boom—I'm afraid the excess money created by those deficits will send prices higher again.

We really haven't learned our lesson. Not completely. There are still a great many people who want more government benefits than we can possibly pay for without creating inflation. And there are still millions of workers who can't understand why they shouldn't have big pay raises year after year. They don't realize that real wage increases—wage increases that don't cause higher prices—have to come from increased productivity.

In other words, we're still facing the same old problem. Too many people still don't understand how our economic system—free enterprise—really works. Unfortunately, that's just as true of Congress as it is of everybody else. In trying to improve the system they often pass legislation that turns out to be a serious handicap.

So why don't we have a simpler system, like socialism? Let the government decide what each of us should do, then divide up the results equally between us.

That's a lot easier to say than to do. Planning the output of an entire nation, then dividing it up equally is a colossal problem. Every socialist nation that tries to do it gets hopelessly bogged down in procedures and red tape. Not one of them has come close to producing as high a standard of living for its people as that which is generally available under free enterprise.

How, without competition, and without the encouragement of profits, and the scourge of losses, could we be sure our farms and factories were efficiently run? And that they produced what the customers really wanted?

How, without the freedom of individuals to try new ideas at their own risk, could we be sure productivity would continue to improve?

Under free enterprise, the decisions that affect the individual are made by the individual. Each of us decides for himself for whom he will work, or whether he will start a business of his own. When we get our pay, or make a profit, we decide for ourselves whether to save it or spend it, and what for.

Millions of individual decisions, added together, shape the activities of the free enterprise economy. People, not governments, determine what will be made and by whom. Practical people, who figure out how to do things most efficiently, tend to become the managers.

Three centuries ago, the English philosopher, John Milton, was a leader in the fight for individual rights. He wrote: "Give me the liberty to know, to utter, and to argue freely according to conscience above all liberties." That is the philosophy behind our Constitution. We believe in liberty and freedom. So why handicap ourselves with any economic system that unnecessarily restricts our freedom of choice and action?

Free enterprise is not perfect; it has its faults. But it also has so many advantages that I hope your generation and future ones will think twice—better yet a hundred times—before you let it slip from your grasp. So far only a very small portion of the human race enjoys human rights and liberties to the extent we do in the United States. I suspect that freedom of enterprise may be a vital part of that achievement.

The rewards and incentives of a free-enterprise system make it so productive that everybody gets more, even the lowest skilled workers. And when they spend their income they find it buys more. The efficiency of free enterprise results in lower prices that benefit everyone.

Why is it that the Russian standard of living—more than sixty years after the Communists took over—hasn't even come close to ours? What's holding it back? Karl Marx thought business profits were a colossal, unfair burden on the backs of workers. Yet, even without paying a dime of profits to anyone, their system hasn't produced a living standard that would appeal even to poor Americans.

Free enterprise—and emphasis on the rights, worth, and importance of the individual—will produce results in any country. Industrious Chinese immigrants to this country discovered that a long time ago. Today they seem to be discovering the idea—flirting with it at least—even in China itself.

Free enterprise has two important weaknesses, either of which could kill or cripple it. One is public ignorance of how it operates. The other is vulnerability to powerful human reactions of envy, jealousy, and hate.

Free enterprise doesn't reward everybody equally. Because of differences in ability, attitude, and sometimes pure chance, the contributions people make to the success of a business vary widely. So does their compensation. Those who make less money frequently don't like it. So they blame it on the system.

Yet even these complainers, whether they realize it or not, are better off under free enterprise than they would be otherwise. Why? Because it's so much more productive. Even those at the lower end of the income scale have more, and can enjoy more, as a result.

But don't expect them to admit it. And don't expect them to stop complaining. If other people are making out better than they are, somebody must be cheating! The system is unfair!

So what should we do about it? The obvious answer, some people say, is socialism. Then everyone's income would be the same. But how would you feel, Peter, if, no matter how hard you tried, no matter how skillful you were, and no matter how many wonderful ideas you contributed, you always got the same pay as everyone else? Would you think it was fair, and continue to give the job your very best? I don't know about you, but to me it sounds like a prison. I'm afraid society— everybody—would suffer a severe drop in production and living standards.

A complaint I often hear about private enterprise is that rich people get too much of our national income, and poor people get too little. But how much is too much and why? And don't forget one important fact: no matter how much they get, they can't take it with them.

Actually, rich people don't consume—I mean actually use up—a great deal more than the average person. There's a limit to how many meals they can eat, how much clothing, cars, and houses they can wear out.

What they don't use up or wear out, is passed along to someone else. If we could save—or eliminate—their *excess* consumption, and give it to the poor, it would hardly be enough to make a noticeable difference in our society. Chickenfeed!

What do the rich do with their excess income? Part of it they contribute to charity. The rest of it goes into savings and investments. That's something our society sorely needs, something that benefits us all—more money for plants and equipment to create new jobs and increase our ability to produce goods.

Being super rich is like having a lollypop that is so big you can't eat it. That's why, when rich people die, and frequently before, they pass large sums along to colleges, universities, hospitals, and other organizations that benefit the public.

When wealthy people die, estate taxes also take a big chunk of what's left. The rich get the same exemptions as everyone else, then the tax rates go zooming. At $1,000,000 the federal estate tax currently hits 49%. Over $3,000,000 it goes to 55%. And there are state inheritance taxes too.

At those rates, it's difficult, unless you are enormously rich, to leave your heirs independently wealthy. I approve of that, Peter. Each generation should face the challenge of having to make its own way. In the course of a lifetime, I've seen more people whose maturity and development were hurt by family wealth than those who were helped. Too much money takes the necessity and challenge out of life. We humans need both to help shape our characters and develop our abilities.

In college you will find some professors who smile deprecatingly at the ideas in this book. You may also hear occasional references to "greedy", "self-interested" businessmen. Many college professors lean toward the "liberal" or "leftist" point of view. They have a socialist bias.

That may be shocking, but really not surprising. In view of the circumstances, how else would you expect them to act? People who work for the educational system are, for the most part, cut off from the profit system. Our schools and colleges, government agencies, and other nonprofit organizations are bogged down in a morass of socialist attitudes. Unusual rewards for exceptional performance are few and far between. Length of service is often more important than competence.

As a result, anyone who chooses these fields as a profession usually has to give up the idea of ever making much money. It isn't in the cards. Teachers and professors, for example, have to reconcile themselves to seeing people of lesser talent and intellectual capacity make more money than they do. That's hard to swallow. It undoubtedly accounts for some of their coolness toward free enterprise.

On the other hand, junking the free-enterprise system in order to appease those who work in nonprofit fields, doesn't make sense either. Their discontent is a problem that has been with us a long while. If there is any quick, easy solution, I'm afraid I don't know what it is.

There are, of course, a few ways an educator can benefit directly from the profit system. One is by writing a popular textbook. If a textbook sells big year after year, the income can be substantial. Incidentally, if we ever hear of a teacher or professor who refuses to accept such royalties, or insists on giving them away to others, we'll take his socialist views far more seriously.

It's fruitless to expect everyone to be happy under free enterprise. To some people, it doesn't make any difference that *everybody* is better off. They don't want *anyone* to be better off than they are no matter how talented those individuals may be, or how hard they may work.

The plain fact is that we've got to preserve free enterprise *in spite of* this opposition. I don't expect it will *ever* cease. But if we let them win—if we let them destroy free enterprise—we'll wind up a poorer nation in more ways than one. They may well destroy many of our personal freedoms along with it.

The reason I wrote this book, Peter, is to explain a few things people need to know that they normally don't learn in high school or college. Many high schools ignore the economic side of life completely. So do many colleges, except for complicated, elective courses in economic theory. But what good is economic theory when students don't understand how the economy works?

This country, and every democracy, need a well-informed electorate. Otherwise democracy represents the blind leading the blind. So study, think, discuss, and get ready. Be prepared to do your part. Above all, Peter, think for yourself. Don't let professors, rabblerousers, or even your own grandfather do it for you.